Catholic Perspectives on

BAPTISM, EUCHARIST AND MINISTRY

A Study Commissioned by the
Catholic Theological Society of America

Edited by
Michael A. Fahey

UNIVERSITY
PRESS OF
AMERICA

LANHAM • NEW YORK • LONDON

Copyright © 1986 by

University Press of America,® Inc.

4720 Boston Way
Lanham, MD 20706

3 Henrietta Street
London WC2E 8LU England

Printed in the United States of America

Co-published by arrangement with
The Catholic Theological Society of America

ISBN (Perfect): 0-8191-5432-6
ISBN   (Cloth): 0-8191-5431-8

All University Press of America books are produced on acid-free
paper which exceeds the minimum standards set by the National
Historical Publications and Records Commission.

DEDICATION

To Max Thurian, brother of the
Taizé community, collaborator in
the Faith and Order Commission,
in appreciation for his devoted
ministry as theologian and ecumenist.

ACKNOWLEDGEMENTS

Thanks are extended to Francis Schüssler Fiorenza, currently president of the Catholic Theological Society of America, for his help and encouragement and to all the members of the Society's board of directors, particularly Patrick Granfield, Monika Hellwig and George Kilcourse for special assistance. Thomas Ryan, director, and the staff of the Canadian Centre for Ecumenism, Montreal, extended hospitality and assistance to the research team. The staff at the World Council of Churches Library in Geneva, especially Pierre Beffa, provided invaluable assistance. The staff of the Centro pro Unione, Rome, in particular Sever J. Voicu, offered bibliographical information. My thanks also are due to James E. Lyons of University Press of America for his assistance.

The final text of this research report was completed during my stay as visiting professor in the Department of Theology, Boston College. The departmental chairman, Robert J. Daly, provided gracious help. Finally, my very special appreciation goes to Linda-Ross Yood who, with meticulous professionalism and indomitable enthusiasm, typed the final version of the manuscript for publication.

Michael A. Fahey
for the CTSA Research Team

CONTENTS

Preface   ix

Introduction   xiii

Chapter I: Genesis of the Lima Document

                         Michael A. Fahey.........3

Chapter II: A Global Evaluation of BEM

                         CTSA Research Team.......9

Chapter III: Twentieth Century Shifts in Roman
               Catholic Attitudes toward Ecumenism

                         Michael A. Fahey........27

Chapter IV: How Do the Churches Read a
               Convergence Text?

                         William Marrevee........47

Chapter V: BEM and New Testament Imperatives
               For Unity

                         Pheme Perkins...........65

Chapter VI: Scripture Index

                         Pheme Perkins...........77

Chapter VII: Lima's Ecclesiology: An Inquiry

                         George Worgul, Jr.......85

Chapter VIII: Faith and Baptism: Sacramental
               Theology in the Lima Document

                         Edward J. Kilmartin....113

Chapter IX: Lima Text on Eucharist

                         Edward J. Kilmartin....135

Chapter X: Lima Document on Ordained Ministry

                         William Marrevee.......163

Selected Bibliography

                         Michael A. Fahey.......187

PREFACE

Michael Fahey, dean and professor in the Faculty
of Theology, University of St. Michael's College,
Toronto, has performed an important service for the
churches and for ecumenism. In 1983 he agreed to
accept the request of the board of directors of the
Catholic Theological Society of America to chair a
research team for the Society to prepare a response to
Baptism, Eucharist and Ministry, the Lima document of
the Faith and Order Commission of the World Council of
Churches. We are grateful to him and to his collabora-
tors: Edward Kilmartin, William Marrevee, Pheme Perkins
and George Worgul, Jr. Their analysis represents not a
simple collection of essays but rather a joint effort
by a group of Catholic scholars sponsored by the CTSA
to help us to arrive at a deeper understanding and
nuanced evaluation of this significant ecumenical
document.

Any statement that stands at the forefront of
ecumenism will naturally not evoke unanimous consensus.
Baptism, Eucharist and Ministry is no exception. Not
only does it challenge some traditional Christian
theological conceptions and practices but it is itself
subject to criticism and challenge. The board of
directors of the CTSA knew that when it originally
proposed this research project and now as it sponsors
its publication. As in the case of previous research
reports of the Society, this sponsorship does not mean
that the Catholic Theological Society of America
endorses every opinion expressed here. This is and
never has been the purpose of its sponsoring research
projects. The purpose has been rather to promote open,
public and pluralistic discussion of important and
sometimes even controversial issues. The board of
directors and several advisers invited to read the
final text judge that the research team has fulfilled
its mandate. The board is pleased to make available
this report in published form.

Undoubtedly, disagreements will emerge. This
research report will be discussed and may even be
criticized from diverse sides for certain positions
taken here. If this does occur, then the report has
served one of its functions. Such discussion is not
only helpful but necessary in the on-going reception of
the Lima document. This report, as the Lima text
itself, provides a central vantage point in ecumenical

discussions from which one can look back as well as forward.

Looking forward is encouraged by significant issues that the contributors raise in each of the three areas: baptism, ministry and eucharist. In regard to baptism, the present commentary points out differences between the conception of baptism in the Lima text and that in the New Testament. As is well known, much of Roman Catholic theology has tended to focus on the theology of the later catechumenate and on the image of regeneration rather than on that of the death, burial and resurrection of Jesus Christ. The faith of Christian communities expressed in one baptism has through the centuries gone hand in hand with diverse theological conceptions of baptism and the Christian's relation to Christ in that sacrament. Such diversity needs to be further explored in future theological reflection.

Ministry, especially episcopal ministry and petrine ministry, is at the center of ecumenical theological discussions. The Lima document and the present commentators also come to terms with this issue. Yet the classic disagreements have within today's situation become transformed. Today new disagreements and conflicts in church life and praxis have emerged. Alongside of disagreements about episcopal and petrine ministry, the role of women within all forms and levels of ministry has become a crucial issue for the future of the churches and for Christian unity.

Eucharistic doctrine is likewise a critical theme. The meaning of the anaphora and of the anamnēsis offering prayer as well as the relation of the eucharistic liturgy to Christ's sacrifice is a complex issue. In this report, Edward Kilmartin, following the position of the Innsbruck Catholic professor of sacramental theology, Lothar Lies, presents a particular theological position that he espouses and defends over against some who disagree with this position. Future research into this and other issues of eucharistic doctrine will require still further research. Among Roman Catholics what needs to be undertaken includes discussion about what the Council of Trent defined on eucharistic teaching, what is the core of credal affirmation on the eucharist, and what is only traditional doctrine or theologoumena.

One of the merits of <u>Catholic Perspectives on Baptism, Eucharist and Ministry</u> is that it raises these and other issues. My hope is that the volume will not be regarded as the end of theological discussion but rather the beginning of further theological research and investigation to help bring about reconciliation among the Christian churches.

The Catholic Theological Society of America is grateful to the individual contributors and especially to the editor. They have prepared a theological response to the Lima document not just for our edification but for future reflection and discussion.

Easter Sunday, 1986   Francis Schüssler Fiorenza
Catholic University   President,
     of America   Catholic Theological Society
Washington   of America

INTRODUCTION

The board of directors of the Catholic Theological Society of America established in 1983 a task force of five persons to prepare a theological evaluation from a Roman Catholic perspective of the Lima document Baptism, Eucharist and Ministry of the Faith and Order Commission of the World Council of Churches. The research team consisted of Michael A. Fahey, dean and professor of theology at the Faculty of Theology, University of St. Michael's College, Toronto, who served as editor and coordinator; Edward J. Kilmartin, professor of liturgical theology at the Pontifical Oriental Institute, Rome, and at Boston College; William Marrevee, professor of systematic theology, St. Paul University, Ottawa; Pheme Perkins, professor of New Testament, Boston College; and George Worgul, Jr., professor of sacramental theology, Duquesne University, Pittsburgh.

The members of the research team met on three separate occasions in New York City, Montreal, and Boston to discuss section by section their global reactions to the document. They also exchanged preliminary drafts of their individual essays for reactions by the others. At the 1984 convention of the CTSA a public workshop was held to give a preliminary report and to invite reactions from members of the Society. During a study period at the World Council of Churches headquarters in Geneva the editor discussed some aspects of this project with Max Thurian.

The participants of this research team do not presume to speak for all members of the Catholic Theological Society of America. They have read initial reactions to the report with interest and appreciation. They hope that this study will be a further contribution to the world-wide reception process now underway in the churches. They also hope that it will assist the Secretariat for Promoting Christian Unity which is preparing a Vatican response to the Lima document. They hope finally that it will be useful to our respective episcopal conferences: the United States Catholic Conference and the Canadian Conference of Catholic Bishops.

Boston
Easter Monday
March 31, 1986

Michael A. Fahey

CHAPTER I:

GENESIS OF THE LIMA DOCUMENT
ON BAPTISM, EUCHARIST AND MINISTRY

Michael A. Fahey, S.J.

GENESIS OF THE LIMA DOCUMENT ON
BAPTISM, EUCHARIST AND MINISTRY

Michael A. Fahey, S.J.

The document presented at the Faith and Order Commission meeting held in Lima, Peru, in January 1982 on **Baptism, Eucharist and Ministry** is the product of fifty years of ecumenical cooperation, first among Protestants, then later between Protestants and Eastern Orthodox, and after the mid-1960s between member churches of the World Council of Churches (WCC) and the Roman Catholic Church. While it is true that even today the Roman Catholic Church is not a member of the Geneva-based World Council of Churches it does participate actively in the formulation of theological statements through formal membership in one of the crucial committees of the WCC, the Faith and Order (Foi et Constitution) Commission, the theological heart of the world organization. The visit of Pope John Paul II to the headquarters of the WCC in 1984 during his pastoral visit to Switzerland underlines the seriousness with which the Catholic Church regards cooperation with this world body today.

The emergence of the Lima document is closely connected with the history of the formation and development of the WCC itself. It is not possible here to retrace that rich history. Others have recently described the various stages of theological dialogue that led to the final formulation of a consensus statement on **Baptism, Eucharist and Ministry**. What shall be attempted here is simply a brief account of the discussions that led to the Lima document, beginning with the first Faith and Order meeting of 1927.

Some of the theological themes treated in the Lima document were touched on already in 1927 at the Lausanne meeting. But there was little progress in the ten years that led up to the next Faith and Order meeting held in Edinburgh just before the outbreak of World War II. In preparation for that 1937 meeting the chairman of the Theological Commission, A.C. Headlam, New Testament scholar and Bishop of Gloucester wrote in the Preface: "(On the sacraments) I do not think the churches will ever agree on definitions, and I do not know that it is necessary that they should." He concluded: " ... it may be quite definitely recognized that no unity is possible on any Eucharistic definition" (p. 547). Only on the "spiritual and devotional" meaning of the Eucharist did he see any reason for hope for agreement.

From the 1937 meeting to the next meeting in 1952 at Lund (Faith and Order III) not only had the first World Assembly of the WCC (Amsterdam, 1948) been held but a shift in attitudes was visible especially among Protestants regarding sacramental realism, a shift due in great measure to the impact of the liturgical movement among Catholics and Protestants. Although the Lund Conference did not dwell on baptism and eucharist for long, it did set forth the christological principle that determines the theological understanding of Christ and sacraments.

Studies on Christ and the Church multiplied in the 1950s, with special attention to baptism, rather than eucharist, leading to the publication of some important works on Christian initiation. But it was especially at the fourth Faith and Order Conference held in Montreal, 1963, that converging thought on Christology and sacramental theology made possible an important report on worship. It was at this time, because of the opening of Vatican II, that Roman Catholic collaboration became more palpable. Still there was no consensus as such. The year 1967 when the Faith and Order Commission met in Bristol saw a significant advance. In the light of the Lund and Montreal meetings and with the help of Roman Catholic, Orthodox and wider Evangelical participation the committee was able to speak of "the emerging ecumenical consensus" on both eucharist and baptism. Four years later, 1971, in the university city of Louvain (Leuven), Belgium, the Faith and Order Commission outlined eight points of an ecumenical agreement on baptism as well as the far reaching text entitled "Beyond Intercommunion." From 1972 to 1974 under the leadership of Lukas Vischer a series of study committees drafted and revised the three statements on baptism, eucharist and ministry.

At this stage the membership of the Faith and Order Commission enlisted the assistance of the Taize theologian, Brother Max Thurian, to coordinate the texts of Lund, Montreal and Bristol into a coherent text. Thurian, according to his own description, stuck as closely to the texts as possible in order to avoid new disagreements. After several years of work this text was further revised with Protestant, Catholic and Orthodox input. In 1974 when the Faith and Order Commission met in Accra, Ghana, it published what can

4

be described as the Ur-Text of BEM, Baptism, Eucharist and One Mutually Recognized Ministry.

An unusual procedure was then initiated. Instead of merely publishing the texts, the Faith and Order Commission asked the Central Committee of the WCC to send the texts to all the member churches with an urgent request for comments and emendations. Over 100 comments were received from churches and theological associations. At Lausanne in 1977 these remarks were then studied and further revision of the text was prepared. Once again churches and associations that had responded were contacted for their comments. In 1981 a homogenous text was available which was presented for discussion at Lima. Further suggestions were made at Lima itself and a final text was prepared for study and consideration of the churches. Some 192 improvements were made at Lima before the text was completed.

It is important for the Roman Catholic community to recognize that Roman Catholic participation at the Lima meeting of the Faith and Order Commission was considerable. Catholics who were present and who participated in the discussion of the text included: Alfredo Altamira (Buenos Aires), Raymond Brown (New York City); B.-D. Dupuy (Paris); Jean Gutierrez (Mexico City); Walter Kasper (Tübingen); Emmanuel Lanne (Chevetogne); André Mapila (Kinshasa); Samuel Rayan (Delhi); Luigi Sartori (Padova); J.-M. Tillard (Ottawa). Two other Roman Catholic members, Michel Hayek (Paris) and Haydée Bouzada (Buenos Aires) were not present but were replaced by M.T. Porcile and F. Bouwen respectively. Three Roman Catholic consultants were invited to participate: René Beaupère, Avery Dulles and Gerhard Voss. Normally Pierre Duprey, liaison member from the Secretariat for Promoting Christian Unity, would have been present but in fact he was unable to attend. Besides the Roman Catholics at Lima over 100 theologians from over 30 countries were in attendance. The churches represented included the Eastern Orthodox, Ancient Oriental Orthodox, Roman Catholic, Old Catholic, Lutheran, Anglican, Reformed, Methodist, United, Disciples, Baptist, Adventist, Pentecostal.

William Lazareth and Nikos Nissiotis of the Faith and Order Commission noted in the preface to the BEM text "that theologians of such widely different traditions should be able to speak so harmoniously about Baptism, Eucharist and Ministry is unprecedented in the modern ecumenical movement." (Preface, p. ix). At the Lima meeting the Benedictine monk Emmanuel Lanne stated that we are now dealing with "a situation (that) has been created which ... is without precedent in Christian history." (cf. Acta, Lima, vol. 1, p. 47).

From this brief overview of the genesis of the Lima document Baptism, Eucharist and Ministry one can appreciate the meticulous care that went into its preparation by numerous churches. The responses by the Roman Catholic Church as well as by other churches have respected the seriousness of the lengthy collaboration.

CHAPTER II:

A GLOBAL EVALUATION OF
BAPTISM, EUCHARIST AND MINISTRY

The CTSA Research Team

A GLOBAL EVALUATION OF
BAPTISM, EUCHARIST AND MINISTRY

The CTSA Research Team

What follows is a summary of conclusions regarding
the BEM text that took shape during our discussions as
a group and as we composed our individual essays. This
evaluation tries to highlight what, for the most part,
is already contained in the essays which were composed
first. In a sense this section aims to provide a
global and more succinct view. It will need to be
read, however, in conjunction with the more detailed
studies of specific issues.

Some official responses to BEM have structured
their statements in order of the four questions asked
in BEM's preface concerning: the extent to which one's
church can recognize here the faith of the Church
through the ages; the consequences that one's church
can draw from BEM for relations with other churches,
particularly those which recognize this as an expression of apostolic faith; the guidance that one's
church can take from this text for worship and education, as well as for ethical and spiritual matters; and
finally, consequences that bear upon the project now
underway, namely the preparation of a common expression
of the apostolic faith for today. Our résumé does not
subdivide remarks according to those four questions
inasmuch as we found too much overlapping. But the
implications should be obvious. It will be clear that
we agree that we recognize in BEM the faith of the
Church through the ages. This report, by its nature,
tends to focus more on certain reservations and hesitations about specific points. We have not always spelt
out our agreements or endorsements of particular
formulations, but they are numerous, sometimes even
enthusiastic.

The BEM document is a remarkable declaration that
has stimulated much theological reflection and deepening of faith not only at the professional level, but
also among non-specialists in local Christian communities. It is widely used, especially in countries
that are confessionally mixed, as discussion material
for study days for clergy, seminarians, laypersons.
Without pretending to be a full-blown treatise of
theology it does give a fresh and thought-provoking
presentation of many central aspects of the Christian
kerygma. BEM tries to attend carefully to the biblical
message. In some places at least it relies on analysis

of liturgical prayers of various churches as a source of theological reflection. It is an encouraging sign that many Christians from different confessions have composed this text after years of labor and have submitted it to their respective churches for consideration and approval. In our view BEM creatively balances a variety of confessional and theological emphases of different Christian traditions. We too, as other commentators, might wish to reformulate certain paragraphs or sentences in different accents or terms. But our own sense is that all this refers not to concerns about faith but rather about theological and exegetical matters of clarification which are not critical from a credal point of view. We record some uneasiness about certain juxtapositions, certain terminological expressions, omissions or exaggerations. But we do not believe that the Christian faith is distorted.

Some drawbacks to the BEM document as a whole must be noted. Because the three segments of the whole document have distinct and separate origins they do not always mesh well. Elements in one section are occasionally presented as isolated entities. There is some regretable lack of cross-referencing from one section to another. Sometimes an insight is expressed better in one section than in another. Slightly different tendencies or emphases can be noted, as for instance, the ecclesial dimension in the ministry section is more nuanced than in the text on baptism. Roman Catholics, however, should not forget that the same phenomenon is observable and sometimes more dramatically, even in various conciliar constitutions and decrees of Vatican II. Such unevenness is inevitable if the texts originate in committees. The marvel is that this unevenness is not more notable.

Our research team noted, as have others, that biblical texts are cited to "prove" more than they sometimes can at the level of historically sensitive exegesis. But again this is not an uncommon practice and is found in preaching, catechetical instruction and even in conciliar or papal teaching. This is true because the Church feels free to cite Scripture in a meditative, allusive way, beyond the limits of the historico-critical method by a sort of instinctive appeal to the "analogy of faith." There is no explicit statement on the fact that some of the situations addressed by New Testament writers are in fact quite distinct from issues of the modern church. Sometimes diverse theological (but complementary) New Testament

10

texts are presented in a monochromatic fashion, blur-
ring the original theological perspectives. Despite
our dissatisfaction from a scholarly viewpoint with the
noncontextual use of Scripture, we did not find dis-
tortion in conclusions drawn from this Scripture.

Some Roman Catholic readers may find unusual the
stress on local church, especially at the congregational or parish level, rather than on one church of
world-wide fellowship served by a ministry of coordina-
tion. Vatican II did in fact endorse greater stress on
the local church but this was seen more as the diocesan
church centered about the bishop. What Vatican II did
say also was that the ministry of bishops acting as a
"college" includes their responsibilities not only at
home but in church matters that have global ramifications. This latter concern is not developed in the
Lima document.

Some views in the document reflect certain
"Catholicizing" tendencies to which our church attaches
particular importance. These tendencies include the
importance attached to the historic episcopate, the
three-fold division of ordained ministry, the encouragement of frequent eucharistic celebrations. These
emphases which appear as natural to us as Catholics
will doubtlessly raise issues with Christians from free
churches organized along more congregational lines.

Since Vatican II the Roman Catholic Church has
been involved in a number of bilateral conversations
and dialogues but far less with multilateral discussions such as the BEM document reflects. Hence as a
church we are less experienced in dealing with the
larger and mixed groups of Christians. This may well
be reflected in the process of official "reception"
which may cause some discomfort for our church leaders.

Before advancing to comments on the three major
sections of BEM it is well to emphasize again that the
text does not deal with a complete theological,
sacramental treatise of the three rituals and liturgies
but focuses on specific issues that historically have
led to divisions. We remind our readers too that BEM
will ultimately have to be seen in conjunction with two
further projects that the Faith and Order Commission
has undertaken, namely, a common formulation of the
apostolic faith for today, and a study to determine
common structures of decision-making in our churches.

11

Whether the Roman Catholic Church should possess full membership in the World Council of Churches as such remains an issue about which there is no clear consensus in our church especially among those charged in our midst with decision-making. Some of the hesitations are of a practical rather than of a theoretical nature. The Vatican seems to prefer for the time being more involvement at the local level through national councils of churches. Catholics are fortunate indeed that they have been invited by the Faith and Order Commission to full partnership in that office. This opportunity is one for which the Roman Catholic Church needs to be especially grateful, especially the chance to participate in the writing of the BEM document.

As a research team of the Catholic Theological Society of America we know, of course, that we do not speak for the Roman Catholic Church nor indeed for all the members of our own Society. Some CTSA members have submitted written reactions to the BEM document; others participated in a seminar held at the CTSA convention in 1984. For our study we have drawn upon skills acquired and training received as Catholic sacramentologists, ecclesiologists and biblical exegetes. We have consulted widely in theological publications by Catholics and other Christians and tried to be guided by the insights of others.

Given the highly complex structures of the modern Roman Catholic Church and the sometimes cumbersome mechanisms for gathering reactions world-wide so that various Vatican agencies can advise how best to prepare "official reaction" at the highest level of authority, we can not expect that this task will progress rapidly. We are encouraged that the Secretariat for Promoting Christian Unity has been requested to prepare an important assessment and evaluation of BEM which will be based on invited submissions from Roman Catholic episcopal conferences, diocesan ecumenical associations, theological faculties and individual theologians. Since this kind of participatory consultation does not have a long history in our own communion one can surely expect difficulties. As Roman Catholics we ask our dialogue partners for patience in a process which for us is slow. Delays do not imply lack of interest.

BAPTISM

The baptism section of BEM aims to draw together
into a whole the many-faceted strands in the New
Testament that describe the meaning of baptism in
Christ. The Lima text does not always attend to the
specific theological perspectives of the New Testament
writers. Still BEM correctly situates the practice of
baptism in the ministry of Jesus. The text then lists
as effects of baptism: participation in Christ's death
and resurrection, pardoning and cleansing from sin, the
gift of the Spirit, incorporation into the body of
Christ, and expression of the sign of the kingdom.
Baptism is administered in water and in the name of the
Trinity. By its nature baptism is an unrepeatable act.
Although drawing upon biblical texts in the baptism
section of BEM, the drafters have not attended much to
the baptismal liturgical rituals of the churches which
shed much light on what the Church confesses. The
biblical section for baptism (B2-7) is considerably
shorter than the corresponding scriptural section for
eucharist (E2-26). Baptism is shown to have been,
throughout the history of the Church, a rite of commitment to the Lord who bestows grace upon individuals.
Baptism is seen as a ritual form expressing God's offer
of salvation.

Even in the biblical sections, however, there is
insufficient attention paid to the ecclesial character
of baptism, that is to say, to the importance of the
Church in the administration and nurturing of baptism.
True, the text does state that baptism unites the
individual to the Church (B6) but this is somewhat
secondary by comparison to the individual's union with
Christ. Entrance into baptism effects unity with
Christ but it is well to stress also that it effects a
common discipleship and extends a call to overcome
divisions. The text needs to emphasize more that
baptism is contextualized by the liturgical and corporate life of the community. Especially in those parts
that treat the relationship of baptism to Christ's
mystery, to conversion, to the gift of the Spirit, and
to confirmation, the ecclesial dimension of baptism in
the text remains in the background. The Church's
instrumentality in bringing about the union of the
baptized with Christ is only fleetingly mentioned.

In the baptism section the title preferred for the
Church is "body of Christ" rather than communitarian
images such as the people of God in Christ. In both

13

forms of baptism, believers' baptism and infant baptism, the context is ecclesial. Especially in the case of infant baptism the role of the Church's faith needs expanding.

Sections that treat the relationship between baptism and faith (B8-10) are correct but fall short of all one might hope to see here. The focus on baptism rather than on "sacrament(s) of initiation" presents some inconveniences. Also, the reasons why Christians in the West separated the administration of baptism from confirmation (chrismation) are not explained. Without some kind of clarification a false impression might be created that those churches which do separate the two stages of Christian initiation believe that the Spirit is not given at baptism but only at the time of confirmation.

Since Roman Catholics will undoubtedly be taken aback by the admonition to the effect that "those churches which baptize children but refuse them a share in the eucharist before such a rite [as confirmation] may wish to ponder whether they have fully appreciated and accepted the consequences of baptism." (Com B14). Catholics would be hard put to conceive of this postponement as a deprivation of the eucharist. Children are prepared for communion gradually before the age of reason, an age seen to be the time when they can respond to faith in Christ in a very personal way. Today this usually precedes confirmation. Catholics are generally convinced that this temporal separation, when accompanied with careful catechesis, is an effective pastoral way of providing for the nurturing process about which the document speaks.

Roman Catholics will regret the failure to mention the catechumenate in the BEM document, such as found in the practice of the restored rite of Christian Initiation for Adults. This restoration has proved to be pastorally and pedagogically effective.

Roman Catholics who are professional theologians, historians and exegetes will understand the reasons for BEM's omitting reference to original sin in conjunction with the conferral of baptism. The connection between the practice of infant baptism and the doctrine of original sin has created problems. Still, given the history of this association in the churches since the time of Augustine of Hippo and given the importance that it still assumes for some, mention should be made of this association if for no other reason than to correct misconceptions. Roman Catholics will need to address this question in their catechesis, along with the history of the doctrine of limbo.

The terminology for the two distinct baptismal practices: baptism of infants and believers' baptism, as they are called in the English translation needs some attention. We are uncomfortable with the expression "believers' baptism" (as with the German equivalent Gläubigentaufe) and we would prefer something closer to what the French edition of BEM uses: baptême des adultes. The juxtaposition of believers and infants in Com B12 suggests that infants are baptized apart from a faith context. This is a regrettable reading based on a misunderstanding. We recognize that the term "adult baptism" does not account for the fact that some "believers" are not yet adults, if they are youths of 10 or 12 years of age. An alternative, even if somewhat cumbersome, is to use the circumlocution: baptism of those who have already personally confessed Jesus as Lord.

The BEM document tries to go beyond the normal explanation of the debate on baptism of infants and those capable of a personal act of faith. The new description stresses the importance of Christian nurture by a family and a local congregation. It also states the need for a subsequent life of Christian discipleship. Hence those who administer baptism upon those who have made an act of faith must be careful to describe this faith not as an individual virtue but something helped by the believing community and ultimately originating in the gratuitous offer of God. These churches may want to practice a ceremony of enrollment for infants. On the other hand the text asks that churches that practice infant baptism avoid "indiscriminate" baptism. By this is meant baptizing without sufficient assurance of an environment in which Christian nurturing will occur. In other words, will the child be raised to appreciate the Christian life? Pastoral problems occur in trying to determine whether a believing setting does exist. All sorts of bitterness and confusion are engendered when a rigoristic and ecumenically insensitive criteria are applied. The practice common today in the Roman Catholic Church of having a baptism planned in advance, even before the baby's birth, is appropriate. Since parenthood is a preeminently teachable moment in the faith-life of the couple, pastors will need to make the most of the opportunity to explain Christian beliefs.

The BEM text suggests that normally baptism should be administered during public worship (B23). Whether it is always feasible to administer baptism during Mass will depend on local conditions. But surely practices such as baptisms in private homes or at the baptistery without the presence of the mother and father, as was previously not uncommon, are to be eliminated. In the same paragraph the BEM text suggests, not without a note of archaism, that baptism is appropriately administered at Easter, Pentecost, Epiphany, as in the early Church. Perhaps all that is intended is that at least some Christians should be baptized at the liturgies of Easter or Pentecost. To postpone most baptisms to those dates, if that what is intended by the suggestion, is impracticable.

The text also states that baptism should normally be administered by an ordained minister (B22). Do the Roman Catholics need to reflect on the baptism of premature babies or babies in some danger or on the practice of baptizing fetuses?

The text mentions that some churches practice baptism without the use of water (B21). For the majority of readers such a practice will most likely be considered bizarre and shocking. More information should have been provided on who baptizes without water or the text should have omitted reference to such a procedure. The practice is not parallel to the decision of certain churches to consider eucharists without bread and wine in cultures where they are not commonly perceived as appropriate food and drink.

EUCHARIST

While the eucharist section of BEM, as noted, is not a full-scale treatment of Christian eucharistic doctrine still, in the space of 33 numbers and six commentary paragraphs, it is surprisingly comprehensive in what it says about the origins and liturgical celebration of eucharist. The text is less comprehensive than the document of the International Lutheran/Roman Catholic consultation <u>Das Herrenmahl</u> (The Eucharist) but it has wider scope than the section on the Lord's Supper in the Final Report of the Anglican/Roman Catholic International Commission (ARCIC). The BEM eucharist section reflects much editing and last-minute changes by a multi-confessional and multi-lingual committee. Sometimes what is asserted is expressed so compactly that it will require careful fleshing-out for the non-specialist. It is hoped that teachers, catechists and parents who use the text will receive good commentaries.

Our committee appreciates the text for its trinitarian, ecclesial and eschatological focus. At the level of faith, the text reflects our understanding of the New Testament and later liturgical and theological traditions. The text emphasizes that the eucharist originates in the promise and command of Jesus. It finds the eucharist prepared for in Jesus' table-fellowship with sinners and specifically inaugurated at the Last Supper. It further states that Jesus Christ is truly present in and at the eucharist where he is host of the meal even if the specific churches cannot explain the "how" of that presence. The eucharist is seen as a doxological sacrifice of praise offered to God on behalf of all creation; it proclaims Jesus' sacrifice on the cross and his resurrection; in it Christians do indeed "offer" in faith, not in the sense that they extend a gift to God, but rather that they recall appreciatively what they have received and continue to receive as gift from God's bounty and which they are offering back in return. BEM further states that the eucharist takes place through the transforming power of the Holy Spirit, that its fruits are both present and future, that it requires that we intensify our commitment to social justice in the world; and that the eucharist is, in a way we cannot fully comprehend, an anticipation of Christ's parousia and the messianic banquet.

To describe the eucharist the text employs the terms thanksgiving to the Father, memorial of Christ, invocation of the Holy Spirit and communion of believers, in anticipation of the kingdom. In all this, the text successfully unifies elements of eucharistic teaching that have often been separated in post-Tridentine Roman Catholic eucharistic doctrine.

In analyzing the structures of eucharistic liturgies the text notes twenty-one elements in all (but the list is not complete)! More notably than in the baptism section the emphasis is ecclesial: the eucharist is the center of Christian worship; it gives life to the body of Christ and to each of its members; it is the Church's act of thanksgiving and through the Church the world's act of thanksgiving; it brings life to the Church as new creation; it symbolizes and realizes the fellowship which constitutes the body of Christ; it is a call for the Church's men and women to serve the world.

17

This text is compatible with the doctrine of the Roman Catholic tradition. We recognize that there are some omissions and differences in formulation between BEM and today's official Catholic teaching of conciliar documents and papal encyclicals. Official Catholic teaching would stress more that the priest represents Christ at the eucharist; it would emphasize the moment of consecration of the bread and wine, elements that are said to be changed into the body and blood of Christ. In some areas, however, a new consensus is slowly taking shape among Catholic theologians which might represent a shift in emphasis or formulations even at the conciliar or papal level. This is not to deny that tension will sometimes occur nor that Roman authorities will not react vigorously to new proposals. What needs to be frequently stated is that there is a difference between the core of eucharistic dogma and its theological elucidation.

Already in the New Testament times there were serious divisions even in eucharistic fellowship. The New Testament texts that appeal to unity are for unity within a small local community and not for that unity we must strive for today in culturally and confessionally divergent churches.

In appealing to the New Testament the text mentions meals of Jesus shared with publicans and sinners. It might have more carefully distinguished those meals from those intended for a closed circle, such as the Last Supper and the post-Resurrection meals. This distinction is needed to explain why the Church feels required to ask that those who participate in the eucharist confess faith in the saving death and resurrection of Jesus.

The list of the 21 parts of the eucharistic liturgy (E27) omits reference to the anamnēsis offering prayer of Christ's sacrifice which follows the account of the Institution. A proper understanding of this prayer is important for understanding what is meant by sacrificium ecclesiae. The brief reference to propitiatory sacrifice as understood in Roman Catholic theology (Com E8) corresponds only to a scholastic, traditional eucharistic theology but fails to indicate that the eucharist includes offering grateful appreciation for the gift of God.

The research team especially appreciated the emphasis found in E20-22 and E24-25 about the connection between social justice and the eucharist. In asserting that all kinds of injustice, racism, separation and lack of freedom are radically challenged when we share in the body and blood of Christ, the text is stating what many theologians especially in the third world have argued.

The sacramental theology contained in this document reflects certain high church convictions. Our own practice as Roman Catholics makes us sympathetic to the recommendation that the eucharist, as celebration of Christ's resurrection, should appropriately be celebrated at least every Sunday. But we feel that one must avoid being too categorical here, especially if this results from a failure to appreciate the reasons for Protestant practices that opt for fewer celebrations. Given the evangelical stress on the centrality of the preached Word, it could well be that eucharistic celebrations once a month would be appropriate for some. We do not favor, however, the practice of some churches which celebrate the eucharist only two or three times a year and even then as a kind of appendage to the worship. One should note that for Roman Catholics in some parts of the world, because of a critical shortage of ordained men which may become more critical, there may result even greater decrease in the frequency of the full eucharistic liturgy every week, and this may well be replaced more commonly by a service of the Word and distribution of communion under the supervision of a lay woman or man.

In attempting to formulate a new language that avoids classical polemics, the text sometimes uses new expressions that, at least in English, are vague and unsatisfying. Some examples of these lapses would include: "The eucharist opens up the vision of the divine rule ..." (22), or, "The world, to which renewal is promised, is present in the whole eucharistic celebration." (23). The statement to the effect that "the celebration of the eucharist properly (normallement) includes the proclamation of the Word" (12) seems much less pointed than the Accra text which argued "eucharist should always be celebrated with the ministry of the Word, for the ministry of the Word points to and is consumated in the eucharist." (Accra 13). Hopefully this first stronger affirmation was not watered down to accomodate the de facto situation in some churches.

What is said about the "right of baptized believers and their ministers" (Com E19) to the eucharist lacks clarity in the English text, although it is clearer in the French and German versions. Since the English text will be the one most widely consulted, some improvement of this opaque passage is needed. The section describing the eucharist as an anticipation of the meal of the kingdom of heaven (22-26) is muddled. In part this can be traced to the fact that the section has been transposed from its original setting in the Accra statement. The transfer has been effected at the expense of clarity.

Our research team is not satisfied with the formulation that states "in most cases, this presidency [of the eucharist] is signified by an ordained minister." It could have been formulated more accurately by stating that in all churches, except those with a strong congregationalist basis, eucharist is always celebrated by an ordained minister and that even in those congregationalist churches, while it is not seen as essential for validity, the ordained person will regularly preside at the Lord's Supper.

Lack of eucharistic hospitality or intercommunion (mentioned in E26) is said to weaken the visible expression of Christian missionary witness, a point that was made as early as the first Edinburgh World Missionary Conference. The reasons why some churches continue to forbid eucharistic hospitality are based on convictions that all Christians do not share in the identical faith. Roman Catholics should be very careful to determine whether they are mistaken about what in fact other Christians actually believe about the real presence of Christ in the eucharist or the nature of ordination, especially to determine whether the difference is only a matter of theological emphasis. Expecting a uniformity of theological expression which is not central to credal statement is certainly an unfair requirement. The BEM text needs to spell out more what are the conditions for practicing intercommunion. Catholics will probably want to move toward decisions about the appropriateness of shared eucharists on a one-to-one basis with specific churches. It is hard to see how this question can be decided without also moving toward the recognition of the authenticity of orders in other Christian churches.

The text mentions as a possibility that in certain parts of the world some other forms of food and drink might be substituted for bread and wine in the eucharist (Com E28). This will surely provoke a strong adverse reaction within the Catholic community at large. In leaving this as an issue to be further

20

explored, the various reasons why one would want to substitute other elements for bread and wine, reasons such as the difficulty and expense of obtaining wine and flour in some areas, or the perception that neither wine nor bread are seen in some parts of the world as appropriate food and drink.

Finally, some remarks can be addressed to practices in the Roman Catholic Church in regard to the eucharist. Catholics will need to initiate some changes in their teaching, preaching and customs if they are to take the text seriously. For instance, Catholics need to stress not only correct doctrinal formulations about eucharistic doctrine, but also the mystery or apophatic dimension of the incomprehensible mystery of the eucharist. Sometimes this dimension is obscured in its teaching. Catholics must inform themselves better what other Christians hold about the Lord's Supper. Among clergy and laity there are many misconceptions and suspicions regarding the eucharistic faith of others. Also, Catholics should make an effort to explain in what sense they understand the eucharist as the sacrifice of Christ and our sacrifice of the Church. If eucharist truly signifies eating and drinking with the risen Christ, Roman Catholic parishes which do not yet regularly practice distribution of communion under both kinds should examine their practice. Catholics also need to look at the practice of accepting "mass intentions" and stipends. One might also raise the question whether the practice on certain occasions of inviting numerous concelebrants does not distract from the role of the presider and even more isolate the other faithful from the central act. The practice in some Catholic parishes of scheduling numerous Masses on Saturdays and Sundays for people's convenience needs to be questioned if one's sense of assembly among the faithful is not to be fragmented. Finally, although this is not an issue raised by BEM, need for greater planning and subsequent evaluation of eucharistic liturgies must be recognized.

MINISTRY

The section on ministry and specifically on ordained ministry in the BEM text is rich and detailed. It is impossible to comment on all aspects. The document begins with the calling of the whole people of God and speaks of the mutual interrelation of ministry and ordained ministry. It discusses the historical forms of ordained ministry and various understandings that succession in apostolic ministry is seen to have had.

The ministry section shows numerous signs of influence from the consensus statements of the bilateral dialogues presently underway both internationally and nationally. This shows that worries within the World Council of Churches about the possible effects of fragmentation from bilateral dialogues are unwarranted. The work of Faith and Order and the work of the bilaterals are complementary.

When Roman Catholics read this text on ordained ministry they should do so against the background of modern official decisions reached in our church about the validity and invalidity of ordinations in other churches. Especially influential documents have been Leo XIII's Apostolicae curae and the decree on ecumenism of Vatican II. In the latter document it is noted that the Reformation churches "have not preserved the proper reality of the eucharistic mystery in its fulness, especially because of the absence/lack (defectum) of the sacrament of Orders." (Unitatis redintegratio 22). The Orthodox are said, however, to "possess true sacraments, above all - by apostolic succession - the priesthood and the eucharist." (Unitatis redintegratio 15). Thus, according to this official document, the Reformation churches, because of a lack of apostolic succession, either lack ordained ministry or have only a deficient one. Translated into other terms this would mean that Protestant ministers are "only" ministers of the Word, but can not preside at the eucharist since, lacking sacramental ordination, they are "not more than lay persons." This is clearly one area where Vatican II did not go beyond the state of the question as it had been formulated in the time of Pope Leo XIII. The time for facing this issue head-on is clearly at hand. Catholics will need to clarify what they mean by the fact that they do not "recognize" the ordination of another. Does it mean that they do not see it as an ordination in their own church or are they attempting to say that the ritual has no effect in another church?

The Lima document goes to some length to spell out the christological basis and the ecclesial context for the ordained ministry. What is stressed is the locally experienced ecclesial fellowship in congregations or parishes rather than in dioceses. This is a new approach for most Roman Catholics. Further it stresses the trinitarian and christological-pneumatological

basis for ministry of the Church before that of the
ordained. In other words the document does not move
immediately from Christ to the ordained minister but
from Christ to the calling of the whole people of God.
This proper and important procedure is stressed by
Catholics also and finds a place even in the revised
Code of Canon Law. Ordained ministry is thus seen as
one of the charisms entrusted to the Church by the Holy
Spirit. The ordained ministers by their function are
said to remind the community of the divine initiative
and of its dependence on Christ who is the source of
ministry. Ordained ministry is not an entity unto
itself but is traced to the specific authority that
Christ entrusted to the apostles. What is continued in
our days is not the actual form of entrustment that
existed between Christ and apostles but the basic
intent remains the same. The sequence is not a linear,
historical sequence going directly back to the apostles
but rather Christ is perceived as now, through the Holy
Spirit, calling persons to be recognized as representatives of Christ for the community.

In the BEM text ordination is not explained
through ontological-juridical categories. It is
described as the action by God and by the community
through which the ordained are strengthened by the
Spirit for their task and are encouraged and supported
by the congregation's prayers and recognition.

Catholics will have to take seriously the fact
that those churches which do not perceive episcopal
succession as apostolic succession and which do not
have their ministers ordained by bishops will not
accept any suggestion that their ministry is invalid
until it is brought into an existing line of episcopal
ordination. One norm which might be used to establish
the effectiveness of ordinations which have not occurred within the setting of episcopal succession would
be one of orthopraxis. Ministry of word and sacrament
would be based on the belief, practice and life of
those churches expressed in another model.

The attempt to resolve the divisions of the
churches over ministry is handled in the BEM text in a
creative way. It suggests a recovery of the episcopate
and the acceptance of the three-fold ministry of the
church (bishop, presbyter, deacon) even though it
admits that there is no single New Testament pattern of
ordained ministry. What is proposed is that the
three-fold ministry serve as the basic structure of the
ordained ministry in a reunited Church of the future.

23

But both the episcopal and non-episcopal churches of today will be expected to revise the exercise of that ministry so that it will be personal, collegial and communitarian in a way that is not the case presently. This would be true for both the local and the regional level. In this attempt there will be effort to retain the benefits of roughly four and a half centuries of non-episcopal experience in some churches so that no insight will be lost but will be integrated into a renewed form of this pattern. The least clear part of this proposal is what will be the role of a deacon in this renewed structure of the three-fold pattern.

The ministry section of the BEM document reflects, from a Roman Catholic perspective, a somewhat underdeveloped ecclesiology. Little attention is given to the kind of communion or fellowship that Catholics have tended to group under the term "collegiality" which points to the responsibility that the bishops have not only for their own particular church but also for the care of oversight they are expected to assume as part of the world-wide fellowship. Perhaps this form of ministry is not developed here because it might raise, prematurely in the minds of some, the whole question of whether there exists or not a Petrine ministry of concern for unity.

There are other central questions that are raised by the ministry text. Among one of the most important is how to face the question of the ordination of women in the Church of the future, and specifically how churches which are opposed to women's ordination would ever be willing to accept them as normal for other churches. This issue is touched upon only briefly in the document (M18) but will clearly have enormous ramifications for the future.

These global reactions to Baptism, Eucharist and Ministry will have to be complemented by comments that are made in the following essays that raise other issues. Our appreciation for the document remains considerable, and we hope that this research project will contribute to the reception of the document especially within our own church.

CHAPTER III:

TWENTIETH CENTURY SHIFTS IN ROMAN CATHOLIC
ATTITUDES TOWARD ECUMENISM

Michael A. Fahey, S.J.

TWENTIETH CENTURY SHIFTS IN ROMAN CATHOLIC ATTITUDES TOWARD ECUMENISM

Michael A. Fahey, S.J.

On May 9, 1980, in the unlikely setting of Accra, Ghana, two religious world leaders met for the first time, Pope John Paul II and the Archbishop of Canterbury, Dr. Robert Runcie. Traveling to Africa to listen to voices in the African churches, Rome and Canterbury stopped to embrace each other as brothers. Their common statement was terse: "The time is too short and the need too pressing to waste Christian energy pursuing old rivalries. The talents and resources of all the churches must be shared if Christ is to be seen and heard effectively." [1] That joint communiqué says much about why the wounds of division must be healed not just between Catholicism and Anglicanism but with the wider world of Protestantism.

True, in our own day, we have seen more progress toward church unity than in other centuries all together. The ecumenical movement in the twentieth century, the commitment to fostering church unity according to the will of Jesus "that all may be one" (Jn 17:21), was originally a movement of the Protestant and Orthodox churches, tracing its roots especially to the famous Edinburgh World Missionary Conference in 1910. At a rather late hour the Catholic Church added its institutional support to this cause. Now there is no turning back until visible expression of Christian unity among the churches emerges. Considerable obstacles remain: lack of understanding, fears, prejudices, timidity, apathy. Seemingly, ecumenism fails to incite enthusiasm in a wide segment of Christian churches. Some Christians are still not even sure what kind of unity they are seeking.

That the encounter between Archbishop and Pope took place not in the splendored, protocol-laden halls of London's Lambeth Palace, not in Vatican suites, but in an African host country was symbolic inasmuch as, to take only the example of Catholics with its 700 million members in the world today, less than one-half of them live in Europe and North America. Countries south of the equator, representing what has come to be called the Third Church, will soon dominate the Christian world. [2] These countries did not launch the Reformation and are impatient with post-Reformation forms of Christianity brought by foreign missionaries to their countries decades ago. They refuse to believe that separation has to be judged a permanent divorce on the grounds of irreconciliability.

This review of shifts in Roman Catholic attitudes toward ecumenism is intended to point toward the future. The stress on tomorrow emphasizes that we can not afford to repeat past debates nor rest content describing present tensions. If we do take a look at what has gone before, this is to help us indulge in visions and dreams of what might be. Even Vatican II toward the end of its decree on Church unity formulated the hope that Catholic and other Christians "will go forward, without prejudging the future inspirations of the Holy Spirit." (<u>Unitatis redintegratio</u>, no. 24).

Earlier Attitudes:

A few considerations about the past are needed to understand tomorrow's possibilities. As is well known, the Roman Catholic Church until recently only tolerated Protestantism as one tolerates bad weather, ill health or error that one is helpless to correct. Rome looked askance on the ecumenical movement. Protestants who proposed theological and religious discussions earlier in this century were tagged as "Pan-Christians." Read the self-assured words of Pope Pius XI from his encyclical published in 1928, <u>Mortalium animos</u>, just one year after the Faith and Order Conference met for the first time in Lausanne. Pius XI stated:

> It is clear why this Apostolic See
> has never allowed its subjects to
> take part in the assemblies of
> non-Catholics. There is but one
> way in which the unity of Christians
> may be fostered, and that is by
> furthering the return to the one true
> Church of Christ of those who are
> separated from it; for from that one
> true Church of Christ they have in the
> past fallen away. The one Church of
> Christ is visible to all, and will
> remain, according to the will of its
> Author, exactly the same as He instituted
> it. The mystical Spouse of Christ has
> never in the course of centuries been
> contaminated, nor in the future can she
> ever be .... [3]

Such a document is sobering and instructive. Its model for church unity was basically what might be called the Prodigal Son model: Protestants are to return in humility, confessing to the parent: "I have sinned against heaven and before you."

In that period Catholics felt obliged to remain aloof from ecumenical contacts to avoid the impression of indifferentism, false irenicism, or even syncretism. Official church documents fostered this attitude. But thanks to the courageous work of certain Christians who had to bear the brunt of criticism, suspicion, even silencing from officials in the church, eventually Catholics became participants in the modern ecumenical movement. Catholics learned to see other Christians as partners in dialogue, persons with whom they already enjoyed a communion or fellowship but with whom they needed to achieve full visible communion. One of the principal voices that worked for this shift in Roman Catholic consciousness was Yves Congar who published in 1937 while only thirty-three years old, his pioneering work Chrétiens désunis (Divided Christendom), a work that launched what one writer has described as The Catholic Rediscovery of Protestantism. [4]

The shift from tolerance to dialogue was faciliated by the shared trauma of World War II, population shifts that occurred after the War, and adoption among Catholics of historical-critical methods for interpreting the Scriptures and gradually even historical documents such as creeds and conciliar declarations. This helped Catholics to put its present legislation and previous diversity into better perspective. The New Testament was seen as containing varying, complementary theologies concerning the mission of Jesus Christ, salvation, apostolic ministry. Some even began to suggest that denominational differences could be seen, in part at least, as expressions of different currents of spirituality that were firmly rooted in the New Testament.

The theological basis for this new openness was Catholicism's belated appreciation that what binds Protestant and Catholic together is richer than what separates. Both are bound together by an appreciation of Jesus' ministry, by commitment to worship God the Father of Jesus Christ, by baptism, by the desire to celebrate the Lord's Supper, and by a shared aspiration to respond to the challenge of the Sermon on the Mount in our modern society. Some communion of koinōnia based on the Holy Spirit's indwelling in the baptized already existed but this invisible communion needed to become visibly expressed. [5] By 1964, the year

29

Vatican II published its decree on ecumenism, it was clear to Catholics that the boundaries of the Church of Christ did not stop at the extremities of the Roman Catholic Church. For, by sharing in faith and baptism, other churches or ecclesial communities possessed a real but imperfect communion in the Holy Spirit. [6] Others besides Catholics, to quote the decree on ecumenism, "have a right to be called Christians and with good reason are accepted as brothers [and sisters] by the children of the Catholic Church." (Unitatis redintegratio, no. 3).

Catholics were now ready to recognize explicitly the charisms, graces and inspirations given to individuals in different historical communities of Christian faith; they were also able to recognize churches, other communities, which form a Catholic viewpoint might be lacking in elements considered crucial to the fullness of church. True a Catholic would not always feel completely comfortable with the way another church might express faith concerning the eucharist, justification, the force of tradition, and so on. But Catholic theologians came to recognize the authentic character of another part of the Christian family. Why? Because the Catholic Church now saw itself as a searching, sojourning church in need of reform. The Reformers, it was now seen, were not to be judged as disobedient, proud rebels, but as pious persons burning with a fervor to eliminate abuses or ambiguities in earlier historical embodiments of the Church Catholic.

Catholic Enrichment through Dialogue

Within the last twenty-five years Roman Catholics came to place greater stress on listening and observing rather than on judging or condemning. (Of course, there are notable exceptions but the general rule stands.) Though Catholics speak with conviction and have no intention of abandoning their own distinctiveness, they have displayed a sincere desire to understand other Catholics and even more to understand other Christians who find Catholic accents, customs and rituals strange and distant.

Immediately after the close of Vatican II the Secretariat for Promoting Christian Unity agreed to the formation of theological exchanges both on the international and national level. [7] In the United States the Bishops' Commission for Ecumenical and Interreligious Affairs (BCEIA) officially inaugurated "bilateral conversations" between Catholics and other Christians.

[8]   An impressive dossier of consensus statements has
been prepared. Though sadly neglected by clergy and
parishioners alike, these texts point the way to what
might be the future of the various Christian churches.
In Catholic libraries or parish pamphlet racks, it is
unfortunately far easier to find copies of jaded
newspapers than copies of these consensus statements.

Out of these dialogues a new theology has been
emerging, not merely on the level of terminology but a
whole new method of approaching traditional teachings
with less prejudice. This theology is more dialectic
in character, more probing in its use of Scripture and
in its appeal to historical events, more sensitive to
changes that had occurred over the centuries, a theology at once less defensive and less apologetic. [9]
Unfortunately the very success of these agreed statements and of their preparatory papers has frightened
off non-professional theologians from daring to discuss
them for fear of wading in over their heads.

Some explanation must be offered to account for
this recent emergence of a new ecumenical theology for
Catholics. Despite the presence of some Orthodox,
Anglican and Protestant observers at Vatican II, that
council was essentially an inner-Catholic affair.   To
produce statements, declarations, and other texts the
council had to move gingerly at times to achieve
consensus among traditionalist and progressive
churchmen.   In the council's exclusively Catholic
setting some complex questions were oversimplified,
overlooked or postponed. Yet in the ecumenical,
bilateral exchanges Catholics had to learn to clarify
expressions that seemed at first glance unacceptable to
the dialogue partner: terms such as sacrifice,
transubstantiation, primacy, collegiality. Of course,
bilateral statements could conveniently skirt ticklish
questions, but they have at least initiated what should
have begun twenty years before the Council of Trent.

This new theology, formulated in an ecumenical
setting, marks a vigorous turning point in modern
ecclesiology. Whereas Vatican II had provided a
sanatio in radice, an after-the-fact legitimation of
ideas that previously had been accounted of dubious
parentage, now in this bilateral forum of exchange, a
new appreciation of the dialogue partner emerged.

The Bilaterals

With regard to these ecumenical conversations, it would be a weird sort of triumphalism if Catholics were to take the credit for discovering this form of theologizing. In fact the roots of these dialogues were rather in earlier exchanges between Anglicans and Orthodox, between Lutherans and Old Catholics, etc. Still it is true that the sheer size and prestige of the Roman See made it inevitable that, when Catholics eventually did join in, the process would receive much more attention.

To summarize here what has been achieved in the twenty years since the first bilateral consultations took place between Catholics and other Christians would be difficult. Some consultations seem to have achieved greater success. Among these would be the Anglican/Roman Catholic International Commission for its statements on the Eucharist (the Windsor statement), on Ministry (the Canterbury statement), on Authority in the Church (the Venice statement), and the Elucidations or clarifications (the so-called Salisbury statement) culminating in The Final Report. [10] Lutherans, who historically have had a rich tradition in doctrinal, credal theology, have also co-authored with Catholics on an international scale important texts: the Malta Report on "The Gospel and the Church," a consensus statement on the Eucharist, and most recently an agreement on justification. This international Lutheran and Catholic group has published a sympathetic analysis of the Augsburg Confession (1530) for its 450th anniversary in which it is argued that the first generation of Lutherans wanted to be regarded as an element within the Roman Catholic Church. [11] In worldwide dialogues with Lutherans it is becoming clear that the classical conflicts between Lutherans and Catholics symbolized in the Protestant trilogy: sola Scriptura, sola gratia, sola fide are being resolved. Those three Protestant "onlies," namely that God speaks to us in Scripture alone, that we are being saved by grace alone, and that we are being justified not by human works but by faith alone, no longer remain a bone of contention because they can be given a highly Catholic interpretation also. [12]

In the United States, Lutherans and Roman Catholics have produced some important studies on baptism, ministry, eucharist, papal primacy, Peter in the New Testament, Mary in the New Testament, even on

32

teaching authority in the church and on infallibility, as well as on justification.

One other international group of dialogues has been the consultation between the Catholic Church and the World Alliance of Reformed Churches which has published an important study on "The Presence of Christ in the Church and the World." In Europe, a consultation between French-speaking Catholics and Reformed theologians has been meeting in Les Dombes, France, and has produced a remarkable series of studies on the Eucharist, reconciliation of ministry, episcopal office, sacraments.

The achievement of these bilateral conversations has been considerable, but there are some drawbacks and constraints. Membership is still far too dominated by clerics, despite the fact that a qualified network of lay theologians and church historians, men and women, could be tapped also. Another problem is how to close the gap between the published high level consultations and church members at grassroots. Again meetings are often too short, some two or three days, at the most, a week. Theologians consult one another, draw up conclusions, all the while casting hasty glances at their return airplane tickets. Some tension has arisen about the question whether church leaders should not give "official" approbation to these documents. If the texts are supposedly so important, ask some, why is it that popes and bishops and pastors have been so slow to formally recognize them as authentic expressions of faith?

In short, what is happening is that in this process of dialogue Catholics are coming to see themselves better through the eyes of others. Does this mean then that Catholics will inevitably some day lose their own self-identity? If so that would be a deceptive gain. What is required is that Catholics discover the de facto pluralism that exists now and has always existed in the Church of the past. For within one and the same adherence to the essentials of Christian faith there must indeed always exist a creative pluralism in liturgical rites, theological emphases, forms of prayer, administrative procedures, etc.

In facing the future, separated Christians must now try to discover whether differences between themselves are based on something negative: tribal sectarianism, pride, cultural isolation, distain for others; or whether differences are based on positive

33

values: respect for a God-willed call to personal freedom, distinctive charism.

The Dominican theologian from Ottawa, Jean-Marie Tillard, has suggested that Christians, especially Catholics, need a new ecumenical approach based on a radical conversion of heart. [13] This conversation will offset the ever-present temptation to exaggerate the importance of certain elements which may well give one distinctive confessional allegiance, but which are not the heart of one's Christian identity. The fundamental "yes" that one formulates in order to assent to belief in Jesus Christ can never be placed, argues Tillard, on the same level as one's "yes" to a specific historical embodiment of Church.

Provided that differences among Christians are not rooted in hatred or ignoble prejudices, then diversities in confessional, cultural, theological traditions may actually be a manifestation of God's diverse graces. In the early stages of sharing with other Christians it may be difficult to identify what divides on the basis of healthy pluralism and what divides because of sectarian isolation. Thus in dialogue one must be slow to categorize too rapidly other views as inaccurate, incomplete, even heretical. Dialogue obviously requires much patience and humility.

Possibly after serious consultation with other Christians, one might be led to conclude that another church has distorted a Gospel tradition because of human shortcomings, historical accident, or simple misunderstanding. But it is also possible, as the Lima document suggests, that one would have to adjust one's own practices or one's theoretical explanation of the faith in light of some forgotten truth preserved in another church tradition. Clearly, Christians as a community have the capacity to discern what is erroneous, what is a miserly abbreviation of a richer tradition. But this discernment of error or incompletion can never be a quick and easy process done by one person or by a small group of similarly inclined individuals. It may take years, even generations of reflection, before clarity is achieved.

Uneasy Feelings

Occasionally church leaders, both Catholic and Protestant, will express opposition to a particular formulation of doctrine in another church or even opposition to a feature of church discipline. They will

34

express a doubt whether such and such a formulation or action is compatible with the fullness of faith, the tradition, or orthodoxy. They will even, at times, take disciplinary actions to assure unity within their own church while questions are under discussion. These restrictive steps are never meant to close off further reflection and mature discussion, but are rather an expression of vigilance regarding the "deposit of faith."

Today many Catholics are confused by a bewildering number of directives, instructions or conclusions made by church officials and quickly distributed by the world press. Believers experience confusion, disorientation, frustration, impatience. For some, changes are too slow; for others, changes are too radical. Some convinced and dedicated persons perceive changes not as a sign of renewal, but a disconcerting toleration of questionable forces, a decline in the standards of authority, a turning away from self-abnegation, a watering down of doctrines, an unhealthy compromise with the value system of secular society. Indeed all these perceptions or some of them could be correct. But the emergence of these feelings among some Catholics, some of whom might even be cardinals or bishops, poses a critical pastoral problem that needs addressing.

In discussion it would have to be stressed that fidelity to the past does not consist simply in repeating forms of the past. One of the most radical expressions of fidelity to the tradition may ironically be change! There do exist definite limits to what can be changed in the faith of the Church. But at the same time the Church must be an intelligible sign to believers and potentially at least to unbelievers, a sign of Christ's presence in the world. How to explain this vocation to those who are confused, how to assist the confused to tolerate and even welcome change, are challenges that merit high priority in the Christian community today.

When the full plenary session of the Secretariat for Promoting Christian Unity held its annual meeting in Rome during 1978 to study the various bilateral consensus statements that had been drawn up to the present, the Secretariat's prefect, Cardinal Jan Willebrands raised the question about what to do with the various consensus statements. The Cardinal reported two separate reactions from people who wanted to end the dialogues. Some activist groups felt that such academic discussions were only a brake to action, that they dowsed cold water on the enthusiasm for Christian unity, because they are excessively prudent. A second group, including some bishops, felt that the church has now copious material for study and so now in peace and quiet (and confessional isolation perhaps) one should sit back and analyze this data at leisure. The Cardinal and the Secretariat rejected both approaches and favored rather continuing the work that needs to be achieved. [14]

What remains ahead, what can we expect from tomorrow, what kind of unity will we be seeking?

Towards Tomorrow

As Christians move toward visible unity, they will need to clarify what exactly is the unity they seek. Is it a sort of merger as between two banks after which one effectively gets absorbed into the other? What then is the nature of the unity we seek? Is it organic union? The goal is illustrated from the experience of a symphony orchestra. A symphony orchestra is formed by a conductor who allows each musician to play appropriately. The conductor does not create the talent nor the sounds, but helps them to blend into a oneness. The unity that we seek today was spelled out forcefully in a WCC consultation held during 1973 at Salamanca concerning "conciliar fellowship." By this understanding the one Church is envisaged as a conciliar fellowship of particular churches which are themselves united. In conciliar fellowship each local church possesses an expression of Christianity in communion with the others. Each witnesses to the same apostolic faith and each recognizes the other church as belonging to the same Church of Jesus Christ. In other words conciliar fellowship would be a communion of communions or a church of churches. The goal would be unity, not uniformity.

One of the clearest expressions of this kind of possible unity was described by the joint Roman Catholic/Presbyterian-Reformed Consultation in the United States. [15] In my remarks about the possibilities of unity in belief, structures and worship, I depend heavily on that consultation's analysis.

Unity in Belief

Christians already share a common belief that Jesus Christ as Lord of history and bearer of salvation has been sent by the Father to lead all creation to liberation through the Holy Spirit. This gift of grace called faith makes possible a response to God's invitation. But faith requires also a certain content, a nucleus of credal sayings. The words we use, the prayers we articulate to express our beliefs may differ, either because they date back to a different century or because they approach the gospel from a different perspective. Many of these faith statements or confessional statements were hammered out in a particular century against the backdrop of a classical controversy.

How can such a unity in belief be achieved? To start off with, Christians need to become thoroughly imbued with the conviction that there is in Christianity, as Vatican II among other voices was to state, a hierarchy of importance to doctrinal tenets, a sort of relative weight to be given one tenet of faith over another. Not all formulations of faith are seen to be as equally useful in every time and every place. [16] The Lima document respects this hierarchy of importance.

Christians currently estranged from one another need a massive re-education to eliminate many prejudices and fixed ideas about the beliefs of others. Previous education, or lack thereof, leads Christians to prejudge others' tenets unfavorably. Apparent omissions or practices judged as curious become more central to the outsider than the deepest convictions of others regarding God, man and nature. So it is that scholars, clergy, religious educators, parents need to assist in the re-education process that alone can save Christianity from further clanishness. The format of such re-education workshops, be they congregational study days, university sponsored symposia, continuing education for clergy, is less important than commitment to openness and change. Gradually there will emerge an instinct enabling persons to distinguish between what is the core of basic belief and what is variable theological or social framework.

Unity in Structures

The term "polity" is often used to describe the way different churches govern, share responsibilities, reach consensus, even determine how to ordain their ministers. In the Christian churches there are three basic forms of polity: episcopal, presbyteral, congregational. Episcopal churches are convinced that the ministry of oversight, supervision, caring described in the New Testament term episkopē, is necessarily carried out today through an institution known as the episcopacy, the collected bishops of a church. Presbyteral churches, not to be identified exclusively with the Presbyterian churches, see authority properly invested in elders or presbyters. Congregational churches, or free churches, look especially to the authority of the individual local congregation for reaching decisions and consensus. The Lima document shows a marked preference for the episcopal form of polity.

There is much more unity amid these various polities since in point of fact few churches are completely exclusivistic about how their churches are governed. With the worldwide expansion of congregational churches there has inevitably been a move toward some sort of worldwide caring that approximates collegial episcopacy, however opposed churches such as the Baptist churches would be about bishops or patriarchs. Churches with episcopal polity such as the Roman Catholic Church manifest a certain longing for congregational self-responsibility, even if its parish councils, local ministerial teams, etc., are by and large not yet successful.

Without eliminating the importance or the value of specific structures that give identity to different churches Christians now seem to appreciate better the force of historical developments that led to their creation. Hence for all the love and respect shown to these institutions they can be somewhat relativized. Unity in structure could therefore never mean uniformity in polity. Ultimately it is better to urge a unity in pastoral ministry, in the kinds of commitment to the needs of others, rather than in uniform administrative organizational tables.

One very promising development toward recognizing a similarity of concerns through a variety of institutions has been the formation of the so-called covenant parishes, parishes that voluntarily are twinned, linked together by a promise of mutual prayer, mutual involvement. Two or more neighboring parishes form a covenant of communion and commitment. They plan common prayers, financial drives, youth programs, Bible study, civic witness or manifestations. Ultimately these covenanted parishes will probably extend eucharistic hospitality toward one another although at the present time this is not officially permitted by Roman Catholic directives.

Unity in Worship

In some visible way, no matter how modest the beginnings, Christians will inevitably move closer to a greater measure of unity in worship. Not every Sunday, but certainly more than once a year, in national or local settings, Christians of different traditions will be involved in corporate worship through divine services of prayer and sacrament. Some existing successes can be pointed to, whether it be shared pulpits, services for the Church Unity Octave, ecumenical services for Palm Sunday, Pentecost or Ash Wednesday. More is bound to come. Churches with obvious strengths in some areas will be less embarrassed to share what is part of their patrimony. Catholic successes in the retreat movement, especially in directed retreats, will spread out to assist Protestant individuals and congregations. The gift for structuring congregational worship, especially through hymns and musical settings in Protestant churches, will surely come to the aid of Catholic parishes that are foundering. Protestants will assist Catholics to learn how music is integral to adoration, petition, thanksgiving.

Further, Catholics can profit from Protestant clergy not only about how to preach more effectively, but more basically they can learn to appreciate how the power of grace is operative when the Word of God is preached in all seriousness. More than tentative, self-conscious sharing of pulpits is envisaged. A common commitment to the study of the Scriptures, to ways of communicating the Word of God today, to joint seminary courses are also much needed. It makes little sense for the official worldwide Roman Catholic Church to join institutionally with the World Council of Churches if at home, in local communities, there is isolation and indifference.

As previously suggested, this sort of sharing will naturally develop into some eucharistic hospitality. This would be the ultimate expression of our conviction that indeed Jesus Christ is truly present when the Lord's Supper is celebrated, not only in Catholic churches but indeed in the various Protestant traditions. Ministers, even if they are not ordained according to the ritual that Catholics identify as the very ancient procedure, laying on of hands by a bishop, could come to be accepted as true and authentically appointed ministers of the eucharist. [17]

Ultimately long-festering wounds of disunity that have marred Christianity can be healed. Unity would be achieved not by a return to a mother church, nor by a merger wherein alternate traditions are evaporated, but by the celebration of a symphony of complementary models. According to this idea first given public expression by Cardinal Jan Willebrands in a famous address at Great St. Mary's Church, Cambridge, England, on January 18, 1970, Christians would learn to regard their traditions as part of a "typology of churches." A model (typos in Greek) would be said to exist wherever there has been "a long, coherent tradition, commanding men's love and loyalty, creating and sustaining a harmonious and organic whole of complementary elements each of which supports the other." [18] The theoretical groundwork for this kind of close association of church models could be firmly established. The stumbling block lies in the reluctance, especially among many Catholic leaders, to accept the practical conclusions of such a new kind of relationship, particularly in the area of the exercise of authority.

The Church of the future will not be a new invention but will be the marriage of persons who retain their own rights, their own personalities, their individual histories and charisms. [19] To the extent that one can peer into the future one can anticipate that this marriage will cause tensions and demand compromises, but at its deepest level will celebrate love, sharing, mutual support. Against this background of shifts in the Roman Catholic community in particular one can appreciate the opportunity that the Lima document now offers.

Notes for Chapter III

1. New York Times, 10 May, 1980, p.1.

2. See: Walbert Bühlmann, The Coming of the Third Church: An Analysis of the Present and Future of the Church (New York: Orbis, 1977).

3. Documents of Christian Unity: Selections from the First and Second Series, 1920-30, ed. G. K. A. Bell (London: Oxford University Press, 1955) 198.

4. Paul M. Minus, Jr., The Catholic Rediscovery of Protestantism: A History of Roman Catholic Ecumenical Pioneering (New York: Paulist, 1976). See also the following useful works: Robert McAfee Brown, The Ecumenical Revolution: An Interpretation of the Catholic-Protestant Dialogue (rev. ed., New York: Doubleday [Anchor Image Book], 1969); Barry Till, The Churches Search for Unity (London: Penguin, 1972); John Macquarrie, Christian Unity and Christian Diversity (London: Chapman, 1979); J. Robert Nelson, "Convergence, Resurgence and Emergence," Centro pro Unione, Bulletin no. 1 (1969) 29-36.

5. On the use of the model communio for ecclesiology, see: The Church as Communion, ed. James Provost, special issue of Jurist 36, 1/2 (1976) 1-245. See also its use in the [U.S.] Anglican/Roman Catholic Agreed Statement, "The Purpose of the Church," in Origins 5 (1975) 328-34.

6. See Growing Together into Unity: Texts of the Faith and Order Commission on Conciliar Fellowship, ed. Choan-Seng Song (Geneva: WCC, 1978). See also, Secretariat for Promoting Christian Unity, Guidelines for Ecumenical Collaboration at the Regional, National and Local Levels [published February 22, 1975] (Washington: NCCB, 1975); U.S. Catholic Ecumenism--Ten Years Later, ed. David Bowman, S.J. (Washington: USCC, 1975).

7. N. Ehrenström and G. Gassmann, Confessions in Dialogue: A Survey of Bilateral Conversations among World Confessional Families, 1959-1974 (3rd rev. ed.; Geneva: WCC, 1975); James F. Puglisi and S. J. Voicu, A Bibliography on Interchurch and Interconfessional Theological Dialogues (Rome: Centro pro Unione, 1984); Stephen Cranford, "An Overview of Recent Bilateral Interchurch Conversations," Centro pro Unione, Bulletin no. 14 (1978) 7-33; "Report from the Second Forum on

Bilateral Conversations to the Participating World Confessional Families and Churches and to the World Council of Churches (Faith and Order Commission)," Centro pro Unione, Bulletin, no. 16 (1979). See also the personal reactions from a member of the Congregation for the Doctrine of the Faith: Jérôme Hamer, "Réflexions sur les dialogues théologiques interconfessionnels," Documentation catholique 70 (1973) 569-73.

8. "The Bilateral Consultations between Roman Catholic Church in the United States and Other Christian Communions; A Theological Review and Critique by the Study Committee of the Catholic Theological Society of America [dated July 1972],"CTSA, Proceedings 27 (1972) 179-232; update for 1972-1979 [dated June 1979], CTSA, Proceedings 34 (1979) 253-85. On the specific bilateral conversations in the USA see the various entries in New Catholic Encyclopedia: Vol. 17: Supplement: Changes in the Church (1979).

9. On the general achievements and future agenda of the bilaterals, see: Hans Kung, "Vatican III: Problems and Opportunities for the Future," in Toward Vatican 111: The Work that Needs to be Done, ed. D. Tracy, et al. (New York: Seabury, 1978) 67-90; Avery Dulles, "Ecumenism: Problems and Opportunities for the Future," Ibid. 91-101. See also: Thaddeus Horgan, "What is the State of Ecumenism Today?" Emmanuel 85 (1979) 11-15.

10. George H. Tavard, "The Anglican-Roman Catholic Agreed Statements and their Reception," Theological Studies 41 (1980) 74-97.

11. Roman Catholic/Lutheran International Commission, "Statement on the Augsburg Confession," Origins 9 (1980) 685-89. See also: The Role of the Augsburg Confession, ed. Joseph A. Burgess (Philadelphia: Fortress, 1980).

12. Karl Rahner, "Open Questions in Dogma Considered by the Institutional Church as Definitely Answered," Journal of Ecumenical Studies 15 (1978) 211-26; also in Catholic Mind 72 (1979) 8-26 (trans. by Michael Fahey).

13. J. M. R. Tillard, "Préparer l'unité: Pour une pastorale oecuménique," Nouvelle revue théologique 102 (1980) 161-78. See his article: "Eucharist, Baptism, Church Oneness and Unity," New Blackfriars 61, no. 76 (1980) 4-15.

14. Jan Willebrands' speech is contained in the SPCU's publication, Information Service, no. 39, I-II (1979) 2-6.

15. The Unity We Seek: A Statement by the Roman Catholic/Presbyterian-Reformed Consultation, ed. E. L. Unterkoefler and A. Harsanyi (New York: Paulist, 1977). See also: John F. Hotchkin, "Probing the Possibilities: The Unfolding Debate on Models of Unity," Interface [Washington: USCC], no. 2 (Spring 1980) 1-11.

16. On unity in doctrine, see address by Cardinal George Basil Hume, "The Churches: How Can Visible Unity Begin? Must Full Doctrinal Agreement Come First?" Origins 7 (1978) 709-13; Herbert Ryan, S.J., "The Churches: How Can Visible Unity Begin? 2. The Path to Unity," Origins 7 (1978) 714-19.

17. Michael A. Fahey, S.J., "Eucharistic Sharing (Intercommunion)," New Catholic Encyclopedia: Vol. 17: Supplement: Change in the Church (1979) 215-17; John Coventry, S.J., "Theological Trends: Intercommunion," The Way 18 (1978) 300-09; 19 (1979) 56-65; 144-53. See also: Norman R. Bauer, "Intercommunion: Possibilities and Practicalities," Ecumenical Trends 7, no. 7 (1978) 97-102.

18. Text in Documents on Anglican/Roman Catholic Relations [vol. I] (Washington: USCCC, 1972) 32-41. For the theological underpinnings see Emmanuel Lanne, O.S.B., "Pluralism and Unity: The Possibility of a Variety of Typologies within the Same Ecclesial Allegiance," One in Christ 6 (1970) 430-51.

19. Georges Dejaifve, S.J., "Hors de l''impasse' oecuménique," Nouvelle revue théologique 101 (1979) 498-509.

CHAPTER IV:

HOW DO THE CHURCHES READ A CONVERGENCE TEXT?

William Marrevee, S.C.J.

HOW DO THE CHURCHES READ A CONVERGENCE TEXT?

William Marrevee, S.C.J.

One of the difficulties which Faith and Order's threefold statement on Baptism, Eucharist and Ministry [1] must face is that all its intended addressees and respondents do not view the convergence statement in the same light. If we look at the various churches, without considering the different groups within them, it is obvious that the degree of importance which these churches are prepared to ascribe to the document will be in direct proportion to the place which baptism, eucharist and ordained ministry have in them and how much, in fact, they shape, positively or negatively, the very life of the churches. Moreover, the attention given to the document will also be significantly determined by the degree of seriousness with which the churches are engaged in the one ecumenical movement and, in particular, what importance they are prepared to give to the work of the Faith and Order Commission as an agent of that one ecumenical movement. What it amounts to is that both the content and the source of the document may be variously assessed by the churches. The responses to the Accra version (1974) of this document which the Lima version (1982) took into account may serve as a first sample of this variety. [2]

But it is equally important to recognize that within the churches there are several interest groups such as the body of believers, the leaders, the theologians, to mention only a few which will look upon the document submitted to the churches from different perspectives. With what kind of presuppositions do these groups react to the text and how do they interact with each other, when they approach the BEM text from their respective positions?

The reaction of the body of believers whose life of faith will be significantly affected if the document has its intended effect is extremely important. But it is questionable how much of a factor a theological-ecumenical text of the kind before us can be in the actual shaping of that life of faith. It might be a sobering revelation if a clear picture of the many factors that shape faith could be established, but it would be surprising if this genre of texts ranked among the most influential.

There is also the difficulty of identifying what the document calls "the highest level of authority" from which "an official response to the text" is expected. [3] This difficulty is only aggravated by the lack of clarity concerning the binding force which such a response would have in the respective churches. Who or what organ speaks authoritatively for the churches? The Commission on Faith and Order recognized this difficulty when it introduced the study "How does the church teach authoritatively today?" [4]

If those in authority and believers in general tend to approach the BEM text with their particular interests in mind, the same applies to the theologians. By the very nature of the text we may expect the convergence statement to find an easier hearing among them, which does not mean, however, that they will be more receptive because much depends on their ecumenical sensitivity and on their openness to the new way of doing theology which is reflected in the document. It is important that this particular interest group not come to the text with unrealistic expectations and that they keep in mind the unique genesis and background of the text. Max Thurian, who has had a major hand in the shaping of the document, has rightly drawn attention to this point. [5]

Perhaps a word of caution should also be expressed about bringing baptism, eucharist and ordained ministry together in one document. Of course, these three realities of church life may be recognized as belonging to the constitutive elements of the way in which the churches live from and hand on the Gospel. Although it is understandable that in the ecumenical dialogues the question of the eucharist has led to a reconsideration of the place and meaning of the ordained ministry in the community that celebrates the eucharist, these three realities are not of the same "quality." In baptism and eucharist, the believing community expresses the source of its identity, namely the mystery of the death and resurrection of Jesus Christ. We touch here the christological center of faith made present among us. Taking note of this fact may, in the light of the Catholic notion of the "hierarchy of truths," [6] have some bearing on the relation of the ordained ministry as a structural element in the church to the foundation of the Christian faith. What is of greater importance to the churches: the Christian identity which they derive from the redemptive mystery of Christ or the confessional identity which they have built up

48

around the forms and understanding of the ordained ministry?

These few introductory remarks are not meant to lead anyone to conclude that the Lima text faces an impossible task. It is simply realistic to draw attention to the many variables that are an inevitable part of "the spiritual process of receiving the text" [7] which the still divided churches have undertaken. The text is the product of a fifty year search by theologians who have matured in the process and come to believe that the document can contribute to the goal of visible unity between the churches. The text has now come out of its relatively safe environment in the Faith and Order Commission into the public forum where it will meet with varying degrees of enthusiasm, concern, skepticism, indifference and hostility. It is impossible to predict its fate. Their enthusiasm prompts the signatories to the document to speak of "a kairos of the ecumenical movement." [8] Whether this is an overstatement or not, the churches' search for visible unity must be influenced by the concrete form the BEM statement, the product of long deliberation, has given it. The churches would have difficulty convincing anyone of their ecumenical commitment if they did not deal with the BEM statement with the appropriate seriousness.

One of the factors to consider in any assessment of the BEM text is the unprecedented character of the document. This is true not only of the document of Faith and Order, but also of the results of many of the bilateral dialogues. BEM is, as such, part of a significant network of convergence and consensus statements that mark the present ecumenical scene. The volume Growth in Agreement [9] is a good illustration of which direction the theological conversations between representatives of various churches and Christian world communions are taking. The participants in these dialogues are entitled to receive some indication whether their constituencies are prepared to follow the path they are mapping out for them. Even though there is a difference between multilateral and the bilateral dialogues, I would like to make some observations that apply to the results of both kinds of dialogue. These observations are part of the realization that the theological dialogues cannot be expected to go on endlessly. Unless some affirmative action is taken by the participating churches, the texts run the risk of becoming one more piece of evidence of a stalled ecumenical process.

It should cause no surprise that the churches and the different interest groups within the churches are ill at ease when they are asked to declare their position vis-à-vis the convergence and consensus texts. Texts of this sort are so new that we really have not developed the terms of reference for this literary genre. For example, it seems to me that the intent of the texts is misread when they are dealt with exclusively as another theological opinion to which the theologian may apply his or her preferred theological apparatus. Though such a legitimate approach might suggest valuable improvements, it could also result in an endless reworking of the text which in the long run would bind no one. In the words of A. Papaderos: "The text has been sent to the churches to be received and not to be reviewed." [10] The text has been composed by the Commission on Faith and Order for the explicit purpose of contributing towards "that experience of life and articulation of faith necessary to realize and maintain the Church's visible unity." [11] A theological response alone would not meet the set aim of the text. The question is not whether we have perfect theological texts before us, but whether the texts are "consonant with our common Christian tradition." [12]

The BEM text has been in the public forum for about four years. Several of the other consensus texts have been published over the last ten years. That is not a sufficient time to measure their effectiveness, but it is long enough for the need to clarify certain aspects of the present ecumenical scene to become evident. This is particularly urgent where doctrinal matters which keep churches from living in communion, but on which there is now increasing agreement among representative theologians of the churches, not acting as individual theologians on their own, but as members of officially mandated joint commissions, are involved. The texts are a new element in the ecumenical landscape and it is incumbent upon the churches to examine themselves in the light of the texts. The aspects I have in mind -- reception, appeal to the apostolic faith, criteria of assessment -- may not be the only ones that need to be attended to, but some degree of clarity or, if possible, of agreement on these will not simply be of help to the various texts for their own sake, but, more importantly, to the role they can play on the way towards the goal of visible unity between the churches.

When there is mention made of reception, particularly in connection with the Lima text, it should be obvious that what is aimed at goes beyond the mere receiving of a text by the greatest possible number of people. With the notion of reception an appeal is made to an important ecclesiological reality that needs to be activated anew in the light of the new situation created by the ecumenical convergence statements of our time, but more importantly by the new relationship between the separated churches as part of the ecumenical movement of which the convergence statements are one of the tangible results. That ecclesiological reality of reception is not only many-faceted, but it also has had a checkered history.

As an important feature of church life its mode of operation is quite dependent on the prevailing ecclesiology. For almost a millenium of institutional-hierarchical ecclesiology, especially in the Roman Catholic tradition, that notion of reception has tended to be predominantly juridical and passive. No wonder that, with the emergence of an ecclesiology that shows more respect for the church as communion, the interest in reception as a constitutive feature of church life is re-awakened. This is not to suggest that the idea of reception was totally absent, but in a polemical and apologetical climate it tended to be very intra-ecclesial. It is particularly historians of the Ancient Church who have shown how an active process of reception was a distinctive characteristic of relations between local churches and made it possible for ecclesial communion to be maintained together with a relative autonomy of the local churches. They also have pointed out the significance of the reception process in decisions taken by councils or synods that claimed to speak for the whole church. This is more than a juridical concern; it is a matter of ecclesial identity by which different particular churches can recognize each other as standing in the apostolic tradition.

There are at least two differences between the kind of reception called for in this ecumenical age compared to the one that was in operation between the particular churches in the Ancient Church. The churches that are invited to enter into the process of reception now do not live in communion with each other; on the contrary, they enter the process of reception

51

precisely for the sake of restoring unity. And the issues on which they are invited to enter into the process of reception, while of a doctrinal nature, do not reflect the doctrinal position of any one church, but a statement of theological convergence that is itself the result of an inchoative reception process between the churches. This twofold difference accounts for an entirely new situation in territory unfamiliar to all parties involved. Part of the difficulty is that the reception process that needs to be entered into now is such that it must complement, if not in fact counteract, a mode of reception that has been prevalent and in most instances is still operative in virtually all churches. In schematic form it could be suggested that an intra-ecclesial reception must give way to an inter-ecclesial reception.

In an intra-ecclesial mode of reception, so characteristic of the pre-ecumenical age, the principal emphasis is on what distinguishes one church from another. If the ecclesiological notion of reception is applicable here at all, it will be appealed to mainly in order to strengthen and define the confessional identity of the churches. It even has a tendency to exclusivity with reference to other churches, which makes it all the more questionable whether the use of the theological category of reception is appropriate here. It would be more realistic to suggest that in that pre-ecumenical age the notion of reception as an ecclesial characteristic was held in abeyance or at most was used in a reductionist sense mainly to preserve the identity of one church.

That also explains the sudden interest today in the way reception functioned in the Ancient Church. Even if the reductionist, intra-ecclesial functioning of it has not come to an end, the ability of the renewed form of reception to become a contributing factor to the restoration of unity between the churches is now being put to the test. The retrieval of this aspect of ecclesial life which has as its principal concern openness to other churches and, more particularly, the restoration of unity between the churches, has already proven fruitful for the theological work undertaken in the various multilateral and bilateral dialogues. Its actual functioning is certainly not limited to the strictly theological arena, but this is where the need to reflect on the concept and to demonstrate its church-building potential has come to the fore.

It would be unfortunate, however, if it merely became a category current in theological-ecumenical discourse. In that case, it would increase the already considerable distance between the ecumenical dialogues and actual church life. The idea of reception does not relate primarily to the reception of ecumenical texts in the various churches, but to the openness between the churches that is necessary for the sake of unity in relation to the common apostolic faith from which they all claim to live. The re-activated process of reception encompasses the whole of church life and reaches into "the deepest life of the churches in their very act of being the Church of God." [14] It is hoped that out of this depth the churches can be brought "to reform, to profound modifications of habits of thought and of work, of ways of life and of faith, whose long status quo has often given the impression of immutability." [15] This is an immense task for the churches, because, just as nothing of church life in the different churches has gone untouched by the situation of division, so every aspect of church life will have to be reviewed and be imbued with the ecumenical will to restore unity.

Appeal to the faith of the apostolic Church

The convergence and consensus texts before us are the fruit of a reception process lived by those who have been involved in their composition. This reception process should not remain the exclusive property of ecumenical experts, but should extend into the very life of the churches. The difficulty which the texts meet in some circles is the charge that they represent the lowest common denominator, something akin to the celebrated phrase: the least that could be accepted by one side, the most that could be accepted by the other. I have yet to see this charge substantiated. Rather than being a conclusion arrived at after close scrutiny of the texts, it is more a disposition to skepticism, at times to suspicion, that prevents the texts from being taken seriously; it precedes and, in fact, blocks the reception process called for now. It should not be interpreted as a manifestation of ill will, but as evidence of a lack of trust that has become so entrenched in confessional identity that it resists the new possibilities that are opened up.

Where does this lack of openness come from? Partly, it may be explained by the method employed in the convergence texts which is different from the method that the divided churches have used to argue the correctness of their various confessional positions. Of course, the fact that in most instances the convergence texts have been commissioned by the churches, and that in all cases they make use of the results of serious scholarship, emanate from ecumenical commitment by the participants and are undertaken together by representatives from different churches, is no guarantee of their truth. But these are qualities that the churches can ill afford to waste. The least one may expect is that they be received with a degree of seriousness that matches the seriousness that has gone into the production of the texts.

One of the chief characteristics of the convergence texts is their appeal to the faith of the apostolic Church. In a sense, such an appeal is not entirely new. All the churches have appealed to the apostolic Church to justify their particular confessional positions. Yet, there is a significant difference inasmuch as the appeal made to it in a polemical and apologetical climate used the situation of division as the starting point. In an ecumenical climate a similar appeal is made, but now the faith of the apostolic Church is taken as a common basis in order to find there the key for setting the divisive issues of the past in a new light with the specific purpose of attempting to arrive at a reconciliation of hitherto mutually exclusive positions.

Is that a manipulation of the apostolic heritage? There is no question that depending on whether one wants to remain divided or whether one wants to be reconciled influences the reading of the apostolic Church. One's starting point and aim are indeed quite decisive, but if that were the only factor determining the outcome of such a reading, then it would indeed be difficult to avoid the impression that, in the final analysis, it is a rather arbitrary matter. But the ecumenical reading of the apostolic Church does not take place in a historical vacuum. In fact, such a reading has become possible because of many factors, not the least of which are the findings of biblical, patristic and historical research. Even if previous generations had been ecumenically disposed, it is no exaggeration to suggest that they were at a distinct disadvantage because they lacked many of the tools now available to reconsider certain claims made in the past. This has nothing to do with a sense of superiority vis-a-vis previous generations. It is a matter of the responsibility the present generation has to

54

seize the opportunity and to use the results of serious scholarship to advance the cause of unity between the churches. The notion of reception is also applicable here and it may lead to nuancing, relativizing, at times even calling into question some cherished confessional positions. This may also, in part, explain the fear that comes over the churches when they are confronted with the results of the ecumenical dialogues.

When mention is made of the faith of the apostolic Church, we are obviously not dealing with a static given. It is a lived and living reality that is recognized as "'the Tradition of the Gospel testified in Scripture, transmitted in and by the Church through the power of the Holy Spirit' (Faith and Order World Conference, 1963)." [16] It has found expression in various traditions that transmit the Gospel. The ancient common traditions as living expressions of the Tradition are particularly likely to become an important catalyst in the process of setting the now divided and mutually exclusive traditions on the path of reconciliation. In this case, principal authority is ascribed not to the various confessional statements of the churches, but to Scripture and to the various expressions of church life that the Gospel gave birth to in the Church's formative period, the symbola, the great liturgies, the great councils, which must be accepted by all churches as authoritative.

The return to the ancient common traditions implies an attempt to find a new language. This is not a matter of simply copying the past, but of finding in the ancient common traditions insights and data which, though never denied, have remained largely ineffective. By re-activating them a new language is formulated that serves to nuance, to integrate or, where appropriate, to challenge and to transcend fixed confessional positions. With this new language the convergence texts attempt to transcend the polemics of the more recent past of separation, not by aiming for an acceptable minimum, but by elevating the mutually exclusive positions to a new common position, at least on those matters of faith where unity is required. At the same time, this new common position will be flexible enough to allow for diversity on non-essential matters.

A good example of this new language are the notions of anamnēsis and epiklēsis, as applied to the eucharist. The reintroduction of these long dormant categories has made it possible to arrive at an

approach to the eucharist that is not uniquely characteristic of any one of the churches, but that allows
the different positions of the separated churches to
come together and, in fact, be enriched.

For is one of the tragedies of the eucharist not
precisely that in the course of its history certain
legitimate aspects have been taken out of their wider
context and given an independence that has made it
extremely difficult to properly relate them to each
other? The issues of sacrifice and what came to be
called "real presence" -- with the virtual exclusion of
other modes of real presence -- spring immediately to
the fore. It is precisely because of their isolation
that they came to be contested and that claims came to
be associated with them that could not but be divisive.

The difficulties surrounding these legitimate
aspects of the eucharist remain unresolvable until they
are re-situated in the wider context of what the church
does when it gathers in thanksgiving to celebrate its
apostolic faith: keeping memorial of the life, death
and resurrection of Jesus Christ. This has nothing to
do with a reduction to an acceptable minimum; on the
contrary, it frees the legitimate aspects of the
eucharist from the reductionism they were subjected to
in the era of polemics.

If the BEM statement has had any success, it is in
the re-introduction and the consistent application of
the notions of anamnēsis and epiklēsis where the
aspects of sacrifice and "real presence" have their
proper home. Because of this the statement attains or
at least comes close to the unity of faith that the
eucharist requires. This may call for a reconsideration of certain practices emanating from the
isolated position of the 'real presence' issue with
which the confessional identity of the Roman Catholic
Church has for so long been associated. Whatever their
legitimacy -- when closely monitored --, these
practices cannot, if we look at the apostolic faith as
it is lived in the ancient common traditions, be
allowed to disrupt the unity in eucharistic faith that
is now within reach.

I have referred to BEM's promising re-introduction
of the notions of anamnēsis and epiklēsis as it applies
to the eucharist. A similar appeal to the faith of the
apostolic Church as lived in the ancient common traditions has also made movement possible in the very
difficult area of the ordained ministry. The necessary
ministry of episkopē has emerged here as the converging

56

factor and, in the light of this, the basic mandate of the concrete forms which the ministry has taken in the course of history may need to be reviewed. It is on this basis that the BEM document makes a specific recommendation and this -- something that tends to be overlooked in various commentaries -- for the sake of a re-united church of the future. The question here is what concrete form of ministry of episkopē does the faith of the apostolic Church demand from the churches for the sake of unity? Obviously, the present forms are not able to maintain the churches in the unity of the apostolic faith. The tragedy is that precisely that ministry which the apostolic Church suggests has the responsibility of maintaining the Church in the unity of faith is one of the most overt factors in maintaining the situation of division.

The need for criteria of evaluation

One of the questions which the Commission on Faith and Order is putting to the churches is "the extent to which your church can recognize in this text the faith of the Church through the ages." [17] That is a perfectly legitimate question to ask, but the difficulty with it is that, to my knowledge, no church has put into place the criteria on which it will undertake to respond to the question. The danger is that the churches will simply resort to the methods they are most familiar with, that is to say that they will assess the convergence statement in the light of their own confessional positions. This will not do for the simple reason that such an approach ignores at least two facts: their own alleged commitment to the ecumenical movement and the newness of the situation that has been created by the appearance of the convergence texts. These two facts make it rather urgent to spell out the criteria on which to evaluate the findings of the ecumenical conversations. The fate of the convergence statements is very dubious until this has been done.

It could be argued, for example, that for the Roman Catholic Church the decree on ecumenism, Unitatis redintegratio, contains the called-for criteria of evaluation. The significance of this magna charta for the Roman Catholic Church's involvement in the ecumenical movement is beyond dispute. And there are indeed elements in it -- one only has to think of the crucial concept of the hierarchy of truths -- that may contribute to the formulation of the criteria we now need, but it is also important to recognize the

shortcomings of the decree. It does not provide us
with the criteria necessary to evaluate the new situation it helped create. No one could have foreseen at
the time that the outcome of the theological dialogue
authorized by Unitatis redintegratio would take the
form of the present convergence claimed by those
officially mandated to engage in dialogue on the
disputed questions. Now that the initial results of
this dialogue have been presented to the churches, the
Roman Catholic Church, and in a parallel way the other
churches as well, must move beyond the decree on
ecumenism.

Such criteria will most likely only emerge by
trial and error. In the absence of such criteria one
can do no better for the moment than cite an example of
how not to proceed. I take as an example the initial
evaluation made by the Congregation for the Doctrine of
the Faith on ARCIC's Final Report. [18] Of course,
this initial evaluation does not pertain to Faith and
Order's BEM statement, but if the Observations of the
Roman Congregation is symptomatic of the Congregation's
way of dealing with the results of ecumenical dialogue,
then we have indeed very grave reasons for concern. My
singling out of the Congregation's response must not be
misinterpreted. I should not be surprised if
theologians of other churches were to detect a similar
trend in early official or semi-official declarations
of their own churches, if these were forthcoming.

It should be quite clear that questioning the
Congregation's response is not the same as calling into
question the legitimacy of the Congregation's assessing
the results of the ecumenical dialogue. Each church
will have to receive the conclusions of the ecumenical
dialogue in a manner that is compatible with the way it
concretely exercises its responsibility for maintaining
the Church in the apostolic faith. In the case of the
Roman Catholic Church, the Congregation is an important
though not the exclusive organ in the exercise of that
responsibility. It would, therefore, be unthinkable
for it to remain on the sidelines of the reception
process. Its evaluation is not simply desirable, but
necessary, if we want to speak of a Roman Catholic
reception of the conclusions of the dialogue.

What must be questioned, however, is the criteria
not spelled out, but in fact used by the Congregation
in evaluating ARCIC's Final Report. In presenting its
difficulties with some of the conclusions arrived at by
ARCIC the Congregation refers exclusively to official

and semi-official positions taken by the Roman Catholic Church during the time that the two traditions have been separated. These positions are being used to evaluate ARCIC's conclusions. But what is called for in the present situation is, in my opinion, precisely the reverse: what the Gospel and the ancient common traditions present on the disputed questions must be received as new light shed on what has been held by the churches in a state of separation. The latter cannot set limits to the former. Nor can the latter simply be ignored. It must be addressed but with the expectation that what is now held in common may complement or modify the unilaterally held positions that are characteristic of the state of division and a polemical climate.

It may well be that in such confrontation a particular church may arrive at the conclusion that it is being asked to sacrifice a much cherished unilateral position. In such a case it will have to be established whether this cherished unilateral position is indeed in harmony with what the Gospel and the ancient common traditions demand the churches to hold. If yes, then the position must come to be accepted by all the churches; if not, then the particular church concerned must ask itself whether it is justified in holding to that position, if in fact the result is the perpetuation of the situation of division. It can also be that the much cherished unilateral position of one church is a legitimate development, but not a necessary development of what the Gospel and the ancient common traditions demand the churches to hold. In such a case, the resulting diversity must be accepted as compatible with the unity in faith.

Must it not be concluded from the sort of difficulties raised by the Congregation for the Doctrine of the Faith that it seems to be frozen in the confessional position? Roman Catholic involvement in the ecumenical dialogue is normally sponsored by the Secretariat for Promoting Christian Unity. Do these two organs in the one Roman Catholic Church operate from the same principles and with the same vision? By raising this question I may be exposing an intra-church problem typical of the Roman Catholic Church. But for the sake of ecumenical honesty would it not be desirable that the two organs try to arrive at a substantial agreement of another kind? It could only advance the ecumenical search or, at least, it would bring clarity to a confusing situation.

Conclusion

These reflections have not touched on any particular detail of the BEM text. They attempt to deal with only some of the aspects that, in my estimation, precede a detailed scrutiny of the text. With what frame of mind will we go to the text? However tentative and cumbersome the formulation of that frame of mind may be, it will have a major bearing on the outcome of any further work. Will that work consist in examining the text in the light of our confessional positions and theological preferences or will its principal thrust be an examination of our confessional positions in the light of the BEM and similar convergence texts?

Notes for Chapter IV

1. Baptism, Eucharist and Ministry (Faith and Order
Paper 111; Geneva: WCC, 1982). The document will be
abbreviated as BEM.

2. Churches on the Way to Consensus: A Survey of
the Replies to the Agreed Statements "One Baptism, One
Eucharist, and a Mutually Recognized Ministry" (Faith
and Order Paper 77; Geneva: WCC, 1977); Towards an
Ecumenical Consensus on Baptism, the Eucharist and
Ministry (Faith and Order Paper 84; Geneva: WCC, 1977);
L. Hoedemaker, "De moeizame weg naar de oekumene:
multilaterale consensus-vorming tussen kerken,"
Tijdschrift voor Theologie 18 (1978) 3-25.

3. BEM, Preface, p. X.

4. "How Does the Church Teach Authoritatively
Today?" One in Christ 12 (1976) 216-39.

5. Max Thurian, "Le ministère et l'ecclésiologie
selon le document 'Baptême - Eucharistie - Ministère,'"
Positions Luthériennes 31 (1983) 269-87.

6. Unitatis redintegratio, no. 11, Austin P.
Flannery, ed. Documents of Vatican II (Grand Rapids:
Eerdmans, 1975) 462.

7. BEM, Preface, p. X.

8. BEM, Preface, p. X.

9. Harding Meyer and Lukas Vischer, eds., Growth in
Agreement (New York: Paulist, 1984).

10. Alexandros Papaderos, "Baptism, Eucharist,
Ministry: Some Thoughts on Reception," The Ecumenical
Review 36 (1984) 196.

11. BEM, Preface, p. IX.

12. Anton Houtepen, "Reception, Tradition, Communion," in Max Thurian, ed., Ecumenical Perspective on
Baptism, Eucharist and Ministry (Faith and Order Paper
116; Geneva: WCC, 1983) 151.

13. On this theme of reception see: Anton Houtepen,
"Reception, Tradition, Communion," in Max Thurian, ed.,
Ecumenical Perspectives, 140-60; Ulrich Kühn,

"Reception - An Imperative and an Opportunity," Ibid. 163-74. Also: Emmanuel Lanne, "The Problem of Reception," in Michael Kinnamon, ed., Towards Visible Unity: Commission of Faith and Order, Lima 1982, Vol. 1: Minutes and Addresses (Faith and Order Paper 112; Geneva: WCC, 1982) 44-53; Alexandros Papaderos, "Baptism, Eucharist, Ministry: Some Thoughts on Reception," The Ecumenical Review 36 (1984) 193-203; William G. Rusch, "'Baptism, Eucharist and Ministry' - and Reception," Dialog 22 (1983) 85-93; Lukas Vischer, "Rezeption in der ökumenischen Bewegung," Kerygma und Dogma 36 (1984) 86-99; Anton Houtepen, "Naar een gemeenschappelijk verstaan van doop, eucharistie en ambt?" Tijdschrift voor Theologie 24 (1984) 247-74. Two theological journals have dealt with reception in a special issue: Journal of Ecumenical Studies 21, no. 1 (1984); Mid-Stream 23, no. 3 (1984).

14. Emmanuel Lanne, "The Problem of Reception," in Michael Kinnamon, ed., Towards an Ecumenical 52.

15. George Tavard, "For a Theology of Dialogue," One in Christ 15 (1979) 12.

16. BEM, Preface, p. IX.

17. BEM, Preface, p. X.

18. Sacred Congregation for the Doctrine of Faith, "Observations on the Final Report of ARCIC," Origins 11 (1982) 752-56.

CHAPTER V:

BEM AND NEW TESTAMENT IMPERATIVES FOR UNITY

Pheme Perkins

BEM AND NEW TESTAMENT IMPERATIVES FOR UNITY

Pheme Perkins

The Lima document **Baptism, Eucharist and Ministry** urges on all Christians the task of achieving visible unity. Such unity is to be reflected in a common faith and mutual acknowledgement of ministries. It is hoped that this process will result in shared eucharistic fellowship among Christians. Were New Testament texts taken in their historical contexts, the BEM document would have to acknowledge that such unity has never existed in anything but a most precarious state. 1 Cor 1:10-30 evidences a community that has been split by baptismal loyalties to the person who "initiated" the Christian. Paul's response is to devalue baptism as an apostolic activity. Instead, he insists that what counts is the preaching of the cross, which engenders that faith by which all persons are saved. [1] Similarly, the appeal to baptism in the insistence upon righteousness through faith as the basis of salvation in Galatians is subordinate to the primary experience of conversion in Paul, hearing the word of the cross and responding in a faith engendered by the Spirit. [2] Baptismal symbolism in the Fourth Gospel is also subordinated to the perception of salvation as belief in Jesus as Son of God. Cleansing takes place through the Spirit or as a result of receiving the word of Jesus. [3] Johannine scholars are uncertain as to which of the divisions in the world of Johannine Christianity are responsible for its reinterpretation of baptismal symbolism. Perhaps, the experience of Christians who had rejected Jesus when faced with persecution was responsible. Perhaps John wished to insist upon the spiritual reality of baptism over against the more naive literalism of other Christians. [4]

The New Testament also contains evidence of serious divisions in eucharistic fellowship. Galatians 2:11-21 reflects a crisis in the Antioch church. Jewish Christians refused to share koinōnia with Gentile Christians. Though Paul insists that the unity of our salvation in the Lord demands shared table-fellowship, he appears to have lost the argument and separates from Antioch and Barnabas after this point. Once again, the Pauline imperative for unity is grounded in his understanding of righteousness through faith in the Lord rather than in a particular interpretation of the meal itself. [5]

65

Paul does understand the eucharistic meal as drawing the boundaries which separate the Christian community from the other cultic associations of the pagan world. Participation "in Christ" implies that the Christian must refuse to participate in religious cult meals (1 Cor 10:17, 21). [6] The solidarity of the new Christian community reflected in its shared meal is seriously threatened by the social divisions between Christians in the Corinthian community. Just as was the case in the social life of Christians, the community meal becomes an occasion for displaying the differences between individuals. Presumably, this display exalted the wealthy patrons of the Corinthian community, who provided the place of meeting and the elements for the meal. Paul protests, as he does against other divisions in the Corinthian community, that the "body of Christ" constituted by the one Spirit, cannot be fractured in this way (1 Cor 11:17-33). [7]

John 6:60-65 evidences another break in eucharistic fellowship among "disciples" of Jesus. The antithesis between flesh and spirit in the passage combined with its emphasis on the relevation of the heavenly Son of Man suggests that the controversy is primarily christological in the Fourth Gospel. The eucharist is not linked with the flesh and blood of the earthly Jesus but with the heavenly Son of Man who is the source of the Spirit. [8] Raymond Brown suggests that this passage goes back to a tradition which reflected the inadequate faith of Jewish Christians. [9] He suggests that Jewish Christianity would reject the sacramental understanding of the meal in Johannine terms, that a divine reality is communicated through the visible elements. [10] The emphasis on the Spirit and Jesus' word as the source of life (6:63) shows that John would be equally opposed to a naive literalism. [11]

Anthropological approaches to ritual and symbolism in the New Testament have suggested that there is a fundamental ambiguity in its symbolization of unity. Baptism, itself, is enriched with all the images available to describe the rite as the Christian's transition from an "old world," life and even "personhood" into the new world of Christ, the Spirit, life, "adopted by God." Baptism is a rite of passage. The person passes through a state of liminality, "disintegration" symbolized in dying with Christ, putting off garments and the life, into a new state of reintegration in the Christian community. However, unlike adolescent rites of passage or the rite of joining a withdrawalist sect like the Essenes, the Christian still lived much of his or her life in the "old world." [12]

The paraenetic traditions blend the images of baptism with moralistic commonplaces about taking off vices and putting on virtues. Yet, the images of new clothing also appear to have been associated with the dream of achieving a renewed humanity, restoring the image of the creator (Col 3:10-11; Gal 3:27-28; 1 Cor 12:13). [13] Exegetes are divided over the question of whether or not these initiatory images carried consequences for the life of the Christian community beyond serving as a paraenetic hook on which to hang a general exhortation to virtuous behavior. [14] For a traditional society in which periods and rites of liminality are part of its social fabric, such periods serve to reinforce the social divisions and boundaries that are rigidly maintained during the "ordinary times." However, insofar as Christianity maintained a strong sense of identity over-against the larger society, it might seek to incorporate elements of liminality into its life. Paul's letters evidence some ambiguity over how this incorporated liminality ought to function. The division of slave and free are overcome, even reversed. Yet, this reversal does not require that Christians free slaves (1 Cor 7:22; Phlm 16). [15] The distinction between male and female is obliterated. Yet, the sexual distinction between male and female is to be reflected in the dress of those who prophesy in the community (1 Cor 11:2-16). [16] On the other hand, Paul is quite insistent that the distinction between Jew and Gentile be overcome in the community's meal fellowship. That effort toward a new unity is represented as a sign of Christ's cosmic reconciliation of the world to God in Eph 2:11-22. However, spiritualization of its religious symbolism makes it possible for the household codes in Eph 5:22-6:9 to portray the new life of the Christian as mandating subordination to a hierarchical structure of obedience and "good order" that inculcates the patriarchal ethos of its society. [17] The social divisions evident in the meals of the Corinthian community also show how little the symbols of a unity expressed in special religious contexts of initiation carried over into the life of Christians.

These examples raise a further question of the relationship between Christian communities and their larger social context. One finds in the New Testament a community which is small, centered on an intimate community life. The language of affection (family) characterizes relationships with God and with each other. The community is shaped around the intimate association of the "house church," with the obligations of mutual concern for each other. It is not, in the New Testament, a cultic society that has been established for the purpose of ritual worship of a god or goddess. [18] Consequently, the underlying identification of Church and ritual structures and offices inherent in the BEM statement will always ring "untrue" to the New Testament. Further, the exhortations to unity in the New Testament are always "inner directed" and usually addressed to small, local communities. Not only does BEM seek to speak to a global Church, it also quite properly, seeks to raise the question of the ethical tasks of the Church in the larger world as they are helped or hindered by the churches' failures to attain unity. Similarly, the BEM document picks up a modern preoccupation with development or progress in the life of faith. The NT, however, speaks of a sharp transition between the old sphere and the new. It then presumes that sanctification or holiness is to characterize the life of Christians in that new community. [19] Attempts to demonstrate a "progressive" sense of sanctification in the New Testament, have failed to find widespread exegetical support. [20]

Even a brief glance at the attached index of NT passages used in the BEM document shows that the use of NT material is mere "proof-texting" for positions that have been formulated on other grounds. Perhaps, this divergence is clearest in the section on ministry. The passages cited to demonstrate the divergent ministries in the NT clearly show that there was no established pattern of ministerial offices and certainly not the traditional bishop, priest and deacon sequence. Yet, BEM recommends that traditional pattern, albeit with a functional definition of the offices. This recommendation flies in the face of the feminist reconstruction of Christian origins, which finds in the NT a model of co-equal discipleship that might help the Church move out of the hierarchical and patriarchal patterns that have dominated its history. [21]

The BEM document might be said to find in the NT symbolic exhortation for the present-day community. It seeks to persuade a fragmented Church that its testimony is seriously impaired as long as the present situation of disunity exists. Our brief look at the NT experience suggest that the call to unity is always something of an eschatological goal in Christian life. Divisions in the Christian community run counter to its symbols of broken boundaries and new humanity. Yet, they are part of the pluralistic fabric of the Church from its origins. One finds a hint of the eschatological nature of Christian unity in the move from speaking about the barriers which are transcended in incorporation into the community (Gal 3:27f.; 1 Cor 12:13) to the future unity of Christians in the one, risen Lord (Rom 6:3-11; Col 2:13; Eph 2:5-6).

The BEM document is quite properly not content with evoking NT symbols of unity, whether baptismal or eschatological. It seeks to invoke the ethical component of the Christian life. Such paraenesis is a strong component of the NT description of the "new life" into which the member of the community comes, though this exhortation is less directly connected with baptism than BEM supposes (Heb 10:22; 1 Pt 3:21; Ac 22:16; 1 Cor 6:11). Both baptism and eucharist are linked with the obligation to embrace all realms of Christian life in the process of reconciliation and the renewal of human dignity. In addition to Gal 3:27-28 and Rom 6:9-10, BEM invokes all of the paraenesis in 1 Pt 2:21-4:6 as evidence of this baptismal obligation. However, this paraenesis is not directly baptismal. It has an apologetic context, which sought to recommend Christians and their behavior in an hostile, pagan context. [22] The fact of an obligation to "good behavior" still requires some critical reflection upon the way in which Christians find the norms for such a life. One finds a similarly "mixed bag" presented in connection with the eucharistic obligation to seek reconciliation and restoration of human dignity. Gal 3:28 is imported from its baptismal context. 1 Cor 11:20-22 is presumed to apply outside the context of divisive behavior by Christians belonging to a single community at their meal. The one bread and cup of 1 Cor 10:16-17, which Paul uses to suggest a Christian solidarity that stands against participation in pagan cults, appears to represent a solidarity outside the boundaries of the eucharistic fellowship. Finally, the logion in Mt 5:23-24 is taken to imply such an obligation to participate in the renewal of human dignity. Didache 14:2 shows that this logion was applied as a rule excluding Christians who had quarreled from the eucharistic meal. One might ask if the obligation for reconciliation is extended to this logion whether the eucharist is properly celebrated at all in a divided and quarreling community!

Gal 3:27-28 appears for a final time in the section on ministry. BEM suggests that it is part of the calling of the Church to convey a new image of humanity. In order to convey this image, it must be possible for "ordained ministry," which represents that community before the world, to be exercised by all persons, regardless of race or sex. But this perception of the "eschatological goal" of human unity, does not prevent the document from accepting church ministries which exclude women so long as those churches are content to permit the validity of women in the ordained ministries of other churches. One suspects that this document is not really inspired by Gal 3:27-28, but by those who worked out the accommodation in Ac 15:20, 29 imposing the kosher laws of Lev 17-18 on the Gentile converts so that table-fellowship might be possible between Gentile and Jewish Christians. [23] And, short of the eschaton, that may be the fate of all our attempts to institutionalize a vision of Christian unity.

Notes for Chapter V

1. The Corinthian community appears to have been divided along lines that reflected various social groups and social prestige. Divisions of social class may be related to the groups referred to later in the letter as the "strong and weak," according to G. Theissen, The Social Setting of Pauline Christianity: Essays on Corinth (Philadelphia: Fortress, 1982) 69-119. Those whom Paul admits to having baptized in this section are among the "strong." They seem to be in tension with the majority of the community who belong to the poorer class. Crispus had been head of the synagogue (Acts 18:8). Gaius apparently had a house in which the community met and had been Paul's host (Rom 16:23). The household of Stephanus are counted among the first converts in Asia and were patrons of Christians in Corinth (1 Cor 16:15). These people are also explicitly mentioned as those who should be obeyed along with Paul's other fellow-workers and laborers (1 Cor 16:16-18). See: W. Meeks, The First Urban Christians (New Haven: Yale, 1983) 118f.

2. Baptism itself does not function as the primary symbol for unity in either case. In the first instance, we have justification, salvation through faith in the crucified and risen Lord. In the second, the Spirit is the basis for the unity of the body of Christ. The Spirit testifies to the presence of salvation outside the Law. However, Paul does not link the Spirit with baptism directly. He ties it to the conversion of the one who hears the word of the cross, that is, to faith (1 Thess 1:4-6; 1 Cor 2:4-5; Gal 3:1-5). See: J. Lull, The Spirit in Galatia: Paul's Interpretation of the Spirit as Divine Power (Missoula: Scholars, 1980) 12. The Spirit is evidence in experiences of the community (Ibid. 25). In both cases, the persons against whom Paul writes consider themselves to be "spiritual." Thus, it is necessary to specify the significance of appeals to the Spirit within the larger framework of Paul's soteriology and anthropology (Ibid. 43).

3. Paul's comment in 1 Cor 1:12 ff. and in the Exodus typology of 1 Cor 10:5, "with most of them God was not pleased," may reflect a critique of an opposing view of baptism. Jn 3:1-15 makes it clear that cleansing is an operation of the Spirit. Water baptism appears in an equivocal position in the Fourth Gospel because of its association with the followers of John the Baptist (3:22-23, 26; 4:1). Belief in Jesus is the

fundamental soteriological category in the gospel. Eternal life is associated with the living water which comes from Jesus in Jn 7:37. This water is the gift of the Spirit that is linked to Jesus' death (Jn 7:39; 19:30). Cleansing is also attributed to Jesus' word (Jn 13:10; 17:14, 17). See: R.A. Culpepper, Anatomy of the Fourth Gospel (Philadelphia: Fortress, 1983) 192-95.

4. The Johannine critique of the sacraments may not be due to an "anti-sacramental" theology but to the experience of the community under persecution. Those who had been baptized and had shared the meal still deserted Jesus. Therefore, the gospel has emphasized belief in Jesus as Son and the love command as the unique marks of discipleship, according to K. Matsunaga, "Is John's Gospel Anti-Sacramental--A New Solution in Light of the Evangelist's Milieu," NTS 27 (1981) 516-24. At the same time, the Johannine pattern of emphasizing the spiritual reality of baptism and the eucharist (giving life) can be taken as the beginning of a genuinely sacramental theology by which the physical sign conveys spiritual reality, according to R. Brown, The Community of the Beloved Disciple (New York: Paulist, 1979) 79, n. 1. Brown indulges in over-interpretation when he presents the healing of the blind man in Jn 9 as an example of baptism as enlightenment (Ibid. 88). Despite the popularity of that view in patristic and liturgical sources, it cannot be defended exegetically. See the discussion in R. Schnackenburg, The Gospel According to St. John, vol. 2. (New York: Crossroad, 1980) 257-58.

5. See the discussion of this controversy by John Meier in J. Meier and R. Brown, Antioch and Rome: New Testament Cradles of Catholic Christianity (Ramsey, N.J.: Paulist, 1983) 38-41.

6. The function of the eucharistic meal in "actualizing" the boundaries of the Christian community is evident in the rejection of Christian sharing in other cult meals. While such boundaries would be presupposed among Jewish Christians, they are peculiar in the pagan environment of the Corinthians, (1 Cor 10:21; Meeks, Urban Christians, 158-61). Paul may have thought that the unity of the Christian community was to be extended to other meals and social interactions between Christians, since Gal 2:12 is not restricted to the eucharistic meal (Ibid. 161).

7. 1 Cor 11:17-33 reflects social stratification of the community meal prior to the special rite of bread and wine, which came at the end of the meal. The earlier part of the meal was apparently understood by the rich Corinthians as a private affair. The host honored his particular friends with special foods while the rest of the community had inferior food or nothing to eat (Theissen, Social Setting, 147-65).

8. See Schnackenburg, John 2, 69-74.

9. Brown, Community, 74-76.

10. Ibid. 78-79, n. 145.

11. J.D.G. Dunn, Unity and Diversity in the New Testament (Philadelphia: Westminster, 1977) 170-71.

12. Meeks, Urban Christians, 150-57.

13. Ibid. 154; II.D. Betz, Galatians (Philadelphia: Fortress, 1979) 186-201, emphasizes the social and political hopes of humanity that are embodied in this formula.

14. Betz, (Galatians, 189-90), notes a strange reluctance on the part of commentators to acknowledge that Paul presents the overcoming of the old social divisions as accomplished fact. He concludes that Paul's ideas do have social and political consequences. Paul's application of them to the situation of Jew and Greek is such a consequence. In addition, the naming of the Greeks first in Col 3:11 implies an abrogation by Greeks of the cultural attitude of supremacy (Ibid. 190-91). Similarly, see E.S. Fiorenza, In Memory of Her: A Feminist Theological Reconstruction of Christian Origins (New York: Crossroad, 1983) 205-20. However, Fiorenza thinks that the formula "neither male nor female" reflects the rejection of patriarchal marriage as definitive of Christian persons and should be taken in light of Paul's comments on marriage and celibacy in 1 Cor 7; ascetic Christian women may have had privileges in worship denied to Christian wives (Ibid. 235 f.).

15. Meeks, Urban Christians, 161f.

16. J. Murphy-O'Connor, "Sex and Logic in 1 Cor 11:2-16," CBQ 42 (1980) 482-500. Fiorenza, (In Memory, 226-30), argues that Paul is not inculcating a difference between men and women grounded in creation but

seeks to differentiate the practice of Christian prophets from the orgiastic excess of pagan cults.

17. Fiorenza, (In Memory, 266-70), notes that Ephesians has replaced the patriarchal code's command to subordination with a variant of the love command but argues that that was not sufficient to halt the development of a patriarchal social code as normative not only, as in 1 Pt 2:11-3:12, for wives and slaves with non-Christian husbands and masters, but within the household of faith itself.

18. Meeks, Urban Christians, 74-89; 169f.

19. J. Saunders, (Paul, the Law and the Jewish People [Philadelphia: Fortress, 1983] 6-9), argues that Paul uses the language of "righteousness through faith" when he wishes to speak of entry into the new sphere of life constituted by the Christian community. When he speaks of the behavior required of those who are to stay in the commmunity, he uses a wide spectrum of metaphors for holiness and sanctification.

20. See the discussion of such attempts to distinguish righteousness through faith from sanctification in Paul by J. Reumann, Righteousness in the New Testament (Ramsey, N.J.: Paulist/Philadelphia: Fortress, 1982) 80-84.

21. See Fiorenza, In Memory, 288-316; 349-51. This transformation of the ekklēsia is not aided by incorporating women into a competitive, hierarchical structure.

22. See the reconstruction of the apologetic setting of 1 Peter by J. Elliott, (A Home for the Homeless: A Sociological Exegesis of 1 Peter: Its Situation and Strategy [Philadelphia: Fortress, 1981] 101-236). Fiorenza, (In Memory, 260-66), agrees that the household code with its exhortation to submission in 1 Peter seeks to lessen the tensions between the Christian community and the larger society. However, she insists that 1 Peter's solution has been bought at the price of abandoning the true vision of Christian freedom and that it made place for introduction of the patriarchal ethos of subordination into the church.

23. Meier, Antioch, 38.

CHAPTER VI:

SCRIPTURE INDEX

Pheme Perkins

EXODUS

<u>24</u>   Passover and Covenant Meal at Mt. Sinai as
<u>E1</u>   prefigurations of eucharist

MATTHEW

<u>3:15</u>   Jesus' baptism as solidarity with sinners
<u>B3</u>

<u>5:23-23</u>   eucharistic reconciliation implies search for
<u>E20</u>   appropriate socio-political, ethical
            relationships

<u>7:29</u>   unique authority of Christ protects the
<u>M16</u>   ministry from becoming domination and from
            isolation

<u>9:36</u>   ministry governed by love for the sheep
<u>M16</u>   protected from becoming domination

<u>10:1-8</u>   authority of disciples from the beginning as
<u>M9</u>   witnesses to the kingdom

<u>26:26-29</u>   eucharist=anamnēsis established by the Lord;
<u>E1; E2;</u>   eucharist as assurance of forgiveness;
E22   eucharist as sign of the final renewal of all
            things which is anticipated in Christian work
            for justice

<u>28:18-20</u>   divine establishment of baptism, triadic
<u>B1; M15</u>   formula; authority of ministers from Jesus
            who received it from the Father

MARK

<u>1:4</u>   baptism as conversion and forgiveness
<u>B4</u>

<u>1:10-11</u>   Spirit revealed Jesus as Son
<u>B4</u>

<u>10:38-45</u>   Jesus' baptism as suffering servant;
<u>B3; M15</u>   ministerial authority in consecration to
            service

| 14:22-25 | eucharist=<u>anamnēsis</u> established by the Lord |
| E1 | |

LUKE

4:18	church proclaims, prefigures kingdom, one
M4	mode is Christ's offer of forgiveness to the
	sinner and healing to the poor

| 22:14-20 | eucharist=<u>anamnēsis</u> established by the Lord |
| E1 | |

| 22:27 | ministerial authority in the consecration to |
| M15 | service |

| 22:30 | authority of the twelve to sit on thrones in |
| M9 | judgment |

JOHN

| 3:3-5 | baptism as re-birth; independence of God's |
| B2; M42 | initiative; ordained ministry as its sign |

| 6:51-58 | eucharist as pledge of eternal life |
| E2 | |

| 13:1 | last meal is sacramental communication of |
| E1 | God's love by Jesus |

ACTS

| 1:21-26 | authority, role of the twelve as witnesses to |
| M9 | the life and resurrection of the Lord |

| 2 | Spirit empowered and united the disciples at |
| B5 | Pentecost |

| 2:42-47 | role of the twelve: eucharist, lead prayer, |
| M9 | proclaim gospel, service |

6:2-6	role of the twelve (as above); diversity of
M9;	ministries in the Jerusalem community and
MCom 21;	Antioch; laying on of hands as the mode of
MCom 40	appointing persons to ministry

| 8:17 | laying on of hands as appointment |
| MCom 40 | |

13:1-3	variety of local ministries; laying on of
MCom 21;	hands as appointment
MCom 40	

13:1-3
MCom 21;
MCom 40   variety of local ministries; laying on of hands as appointment

14:23
MCom 40   laying on of hands as appointment

15:13-22
MCom 21   variety of ministries, Jerusalem and Antioch

19:6
MCom 40   laying on of hands as appointment

ACTS

22:16
B4   baptism as the basis of a new ethical orientation in Christ

ROMANS

6:3-11
B2; B3
B10   baptism is participation in death and resurrection of Christ, image of one reality; will be one in resurrection like Christ; ethical orientation in baptism implies sanctification and realization of the will of God in all realms of life

8:18-24
B9   baptism as living in new relationships while waiting the new creation (growth in faith)

8:34
E8   eucharistic intercession linked to Son as Heavenly High Priest, intercessor

12:1
E10   offering of life as spiritual sacrifice nourished by the eucharist

15:16
MCom 17   sharing the priesthood of Christ

16:1
MCom 21   variety of ministries

1 CORINTHIANS

6:11
B2; B4   baptism as washing away of sin; baptism and new ethical orientation

10:1-2
B2   baptism as exodus from bondage

10:16-17 E20	eucharistic reconciliation demands appropriate realization in socio-political relationships
11:20-25 E1; E20; E22	eucharist=anamnēsis; eucharistic reconciliation implies the search for appropriate socio-political relationships; eucharist is a sign of the final renewal of all things which should also be evident in Christian efforts for justice in anticipation of the coming of the Kingdom of God
12:13 B2	baptism implies transcending the barriers which separate humans
12:28 MCom 21	variety of ministries in the community
15:22-28, 49-57 B9	living out new relationships as Christian awaits new creation (life-long growth)

2 CORINTHIANS

1:21-22 B5	Spirit conferred on the baptized as a promise of their inheritance and to nurture the life of faith
3:18 B9	life-long growth in faith indicated by transformation into the likeness of the Lord
8:19 MCom 40	laying on of hands as appointment

GALATIANS

| 3:27-28
B2;
BCom 6;
B10;
E20;
M18 | baptism as being clothed with Christ; baptism transcends barriers between humans; failure of witness to baptismal unity and persistence of social divisions within the church calls baptismal unity into quesion; new ethical orientation in baptism implies sanctification, realization of the will of God in all realms of life; eucharistic reconciliation demands search for appropriate socio-political forms of reconciliation; the call to convey a new image of humanity implies that we must discover that ministry can be exercised by women as well as men |

EPHESIANS

1:13-14   Spirit bestowed in baptism as promise and
B5; B19   nurture the life of faith; pledge of future
           salvation

2:5-6   Christians to share one resurrection of
B3   Christ

3:20   Spirit sets new forces in motion, opens more
M42   abundant possibilities than any we can think
           of

4:4-6   Christian unity implied in confessing one
B5   God, baptism

4:13   faith and growth into the fullness of Christ
B8

5:14   baptism as enlightenment
B2

PHILIPPIANS

1:1   variety of ministries
MCom 21

COLOSSIANS

2:12-13   baptism, participation in death and
B2; B3   resurrection of Christ; Christians will share
           one resurrection, like Jesus

1 TIMOTHY

4:14   ordination=laying on of hands, invoke Spirit
M39   by those appointed to do so; laying on of
MCom 40   hands as appointment

2 TIMOTHY

1:6   ordination=laying on of hands, invoke Spirit
M39;   by those appointed to do so; laying on of
MCom 40   hands as appointment

TITUS

3:5   baptism as renewal by the Spirit
B2

HEBREWS

7:25
E8
eucharistic intercession; Son as heavenly
High Priest, intercessor

10:22
B4
baptismal cleansing is basis for new ethical
orientation in the Spirit

1 PETER

2:5
E10
offering of daily life as a spiritual
sacrifice nourished by the eucharist

2:21-4:6
B10
new ethical orientation in baptism implies
sanctification, extension of the will of God
into all realms of life

3:20-21
B2; B4
baptism experience of salvation from the
flood; basis of new ethical orientation in
the Spirit

REVELATION

19:9
E1
eucharist as anticipated Supper of the Lamb

CHAPTER VII:

LIMA'S ECCLESIOLOGY: AN INQUIRY

George Worgul, Jr.

LIMA'S ECCLESIOLOGY: AN INQUIRY

George Worgul, Jr.

The Lima document **Baptism, Eucharist and Ministry** brings the ecumenical movement to a new level of discourse and consensus on central issues involved in the journey toward full unity of the Church. The focus of the document makes this claim evident. Baptism, eucharist and ministry are ecclesial actions which symbolize and cause ecclesial communion. [1] The publication of BEM extends the ecumenical discourse on these areas of sacramental life and praxis beyond the committees and documents of the Faith and Order Commission to the actual ecclesial communions throughout the world. It asks: 1) whether the text can be recognized as the faith of the Church throughout the ages, 2) the consequences of the text for ecumenical dialogue, and 3) the impact the text might have on the life of any actual ecclesial community. [2]

BEM is not a complete theology of baptism, eucharist and ministry as one might discover in graduate theology lecture halls. Rather, it is an agreement "on those aspects of the theme that have been directly or indirectly related to the problems of mutual recognition leading to unity." [3] Therefore, the document can not be critiqued in light of vast theological literature on these issues. However, since BEM has been published to invite reception by the Church, an evaluation is necessary. The present evaluation will limit itself to one major issue: the ecclesiology operative in the document.

Contemporary sacramentology views sacraments as corporate actions of the Church which concretize its nature and mission in the world. This vision suggests a point of departure in evaluating BEM. This essay hopes to uncover the ecclesiology operative in the Lima document, specifically in the sections on baptism and the eucharist. It will also attempt to contrast this ecclesiology with that contained in the new Rite of Christian Initiation (RCIA) promulgated recently in the Roman Catholic Church. [4] The reasons for this limitation are twofold: first, the space restrictions of the essay; second, the notable contrast in the ecclesiological orientation of the baptism-eucharist texts and the text on ministry. A critical analysis of this contrast would itself necessitate a separate article.

Theological Presuppositions

Any theological articulation of the meaning of baptism, eucharist or ministry is extremely difficult, if not impossible, without including the Church as the major reference point. Since the writings of Schillebeeckx, Semmelroth and Rahner [5] in the fifties and sixties, the theological intertwining of Christology, ecclesiology and sacramentology has become a modus operandi in Roman Catholic theology. More recent work has expanded this grid to include trinitarian and specifically pneumatological references as well. [6] The writings of these theologians portray Christ as the premier and full sacrament of God, the Church as the sacrament of Christ and the individual sacraments as concrete realizations of ecclesial life and mission. [7] Consequently, the ecclesiology absent, implicit or overt in the BEM text reflects poignantly in evaluating its theological adequacy and possible reception as a statement of ecclesial faith within the context of the Roman Catholic tradition. An exploration of two questions assists in undertaking this evaluation. First, what are the textual references to the Church in the statements on baptism and eucharist? Second, how are these sacraments related to the Church in the text?

Textual References

References to the Church appear throughout the Lima document. The following charts outline the statement on baptism and eucharist with the corresponding references to the Church.

BAPTISM

I.	The Institution of Baptism	"... entry into the New Covenant between God and God's people" (B1)
		"The churches today continue this practice [baptism] as a rite of commitment to the Lord...." (B1)
II.	The Meaning of Baptism	"[Baptism] unites the one baptized

86

with Christ and with
his people. The New
Testament scriptures
and the liturgy of
the Church unfold
the meaning of
baptism in various
images..." (B2)

A.   Participation in Christ's
      Death and Resurrection

B.   Conversion, Pardoning and
      Cleansing

C.   The Gift of the Spirit

D.   Incorporation into the
      Body of Christ

                        "Administered in
                        obedience to our
                        Lord, baptism is a
                        sign and seal of our
                        common discipleship.
                        Through baptism,
                        Christians are
                        brought into union
                        with Christ, with
                        each other and with
                        the Church of every
                        time and place. Our
                        common baptism,
                        which unites us to
                        Christ in faith, is
                        thus a basic bond of
                        unity. We are one
                        people and are
                        called to confess
                        and serve one Lord
                        in each place and in
                        all the world. The
                        union with Christ
                        which we share
                        through baptism has
                        important
                        implications for
                        Christian unity. ...
                        When baptismal unity
                        is realized in one
                        holy, catholic,
                        apostolic Church, a

genuine Christian
witness can be made
to the healing and
reconciling love of
God. Therefore, our
one baptism into
Christ constitutes a
call to the churches
to overcome their
divisions and
visibly manifest
their fellowship."
(B6)

E. The Sign of the Kingdom

III. Baptism and Faith

"The necessity of
faith for the
reception of the
salvation embodied
and set forth in
baptism is
acknowledged by all
the churches.
Personal commitment
is necessary for
responsible
membership in the
body of Christ."
(B8)

"In this new
relationship
[grace], the
baptized live
for the sake of
Christ, of his
Church and of the
world which he
loves..." (B9)

"[Baptized
believers] have a
common
responsibility, here
and now, to bear
witness together to
the Gospel of
Christ... . The
context of this
common witness is

the Church and the world. Within a fellowship of witness and service, Christians discover the full significance of the one baptism as the gift of God to all God's people." (B10)

IV. Baptismal Practices

    A. Baptism of Believers and Infants

"Some churches baptize infants brought by parents or guardians who are ready, in and with the Church, to bring up the children in the Christian faith." (B11)

"Both the baptism of believers and the baptism of infants take place in the Church as the community of faith." (B12)

"All baptism is rooted in and declares Christ's faithfulness unto death. It has its setting within the life and faith of the Church and, through the witness of the whole Church, points to the faithfulness of God, the ground of all life in faith. At every baptism the whole congregation reaffirms its faith in God and pledges itself to provide an

89

environment of witness and service. Baptism should, therefore, always be celebrated and developed in the setting of the Christian community." (B12)

B. Baptism-Chrismation-Confirmation

C. Towards Mutual Recognition of Baptism

V. The Celebration of Baptism   "Since baptism is intimately connected with the corporate life and worship of the Church, it should normally be administered during public worship, so that the members of the congregation may be reminded of their own baptism and may welcome into their fellowship those who are baptized and whom they are commited to nurture in the Christian faith." (B23)

A cursory reading of the above textual references reveals that different ecclesiological dimensions are operative in the Lima text's vision of baptism. Baptism is portrayed as an entrance into the new covenant between God and God's people (B1). Baptism effects a unity with Christ (B2, 6). Baptism brings about common discipleship (B6,8,9,10). Baptism is a call to overcome division and to pursue a common fellowship (B6). Baptism is contextualized by the liturgical and corporate life of the community (B12, 23). One also notices that the ecclesiological dimension of baptism goes undetected in the textual sections treating the relationship of baptism and Christ's paschal mystery, conversion, the gift of the Spirit, and confirmation (chrismation).

EUCHARIST

I. The Institution of the
    Eucharist

"Its [the
eucharist's]
celebration
continues as the
central act of the
Church's worship."
(E1)

II. The Meaning of the
    Eucharist

"In the eucharistic
meal, in the eating
and drinking of the
bread and wine,
Christ grants
communion with
himself. God
himself acts, giving
life to the body of
Christ and renewing
each member. In
accordance with
Christ's promise,
each baptized member
receives in the
eucharist the
assurance of the
forgiveness of sins
(Matt. 26:28) and
the pledge of
eternal life (John
6:51-58)." (E2)

A. The Eucharist as
    Thanksgiving to the
    Father

"It [the eucharist]
is the great
thanksgiving to the
Father for
everything
accomplished in
creation, redemption
and sanctification,
for everything
accomplished by God
now in the Church
and in the world in
spite of the sins of

91

human beings... .
Thus the eucharist
is the benediction
(berakah) by which
the Church expresses
its thankfulness for
all God's benefits."
(E3)

"The eucharist is
the great sacrifice
of praise by which
the Church speaks on
behalf of the whole
creation." (E4)

B. The Eucharist as Anamnesis
of Memorial of Christ

"The anamnēsis in
which Christ acts
through the joyful
celebration of his
Church is thus both
representation and
anticipation. It is
not only a calling
to mind of what is
past and of its
significance. It is
the Church's
effective
proclamation of
God's mighty acts
and promises." (E7)

"Representation and
anticipation are
expressed in
thanksgiving and
intercession. The
Church, gratefully
recalling God's
mighty acts of
redemption,
beseeches God to
give the benefits of
these acts to every
human being.
In thanksgiving and
intercession, the
Church is united
with the Son, its

great High Priest
and Intercessor
(Rom. 8:34; Heb.
7:25)." (E8)

"United to our Lord
and in communion
with all the saints
and martyrs, we are
renewed in the
covenant sealed by
the blood of
Christ." (E11)

C. The Eucharist as
   Invocation of the
   Spirit

"...the Church prays
to the Father for
the gift of the Holy
Spirit in order that
the eucharistic
event may be a
reality: the real
presence of the
crucified and risen
Christ giving his
life for all
humanity." (E14)

"The Holy Spirit
through the
eucharist gives a
foretaste of the
Kingdom of God: the
Church receives the
life of the new
creation and the
assurance of the
Lord's return."
(E18)

D. The Eucharist as
   Communion of the
   Faithful

"The eucharistic
communion with
Christ who nourishes
the life of the
Church is at the
same time communion
within the body of
Christ which is the

Church. The sharing
in one bread and the
common cup in a
given place
demonstrates and
effects the oneness
of the sharers with
Christ and with
their fellow sharers
in all times and
places. It is in
the eucharist that
the community of
God's people is
fully manifested.
Eucharistic
celebrations always
have to do with the
whole Church, and
the whole Church is
involved in each
local eucharistic
celebration.
In so far as a
church claims to be
a manifestation of
the whole Church, it
will take care to
order its own life
in ways which take
seriously the
interests and
concerns of other
churches." (E19)

E. The Eucharist as Meal
   of the Kingdom

"The eucharist is
the feast at which
the Church gives
thanks to God for
these signs [of
renewal] and
joyfully celebrates
and anticipates the
coming of the
Kingdom in Christ (1
Cor. 11:26; Matt.
26:29)." (E22)

"The world, to which
renewal is promised,

is present in the
whole eucharistic
celebration. The
world is present in
the thanksgiving to
the Father, where
the Church speaks on
behalf of the whole
creation; in the
memorial of Christ,
where the Church,
united with its
great High Priest
and Intercessor,
prays for the world;
in the prayer for
the gift of the Holy
Spirit, where the
Church asks for
sanctification and
new creation." (E23)

"Reconciled in the
eucharist, the
members of the body
of Christ are called
to be servants of
reconciliation among
men and women and
witnesses of the joy
of resurrection."
(E24)

"The very
celebration of the
eucharist is an
instance of the
Church's
participation in
God's mission to the
world." (E25)

III. The Celebration of
the Eucharist

"In the celebration
of the eucharist,
Christ gathers,
teaches and
nourishes the
Church." (E29)

A simple reading of the above textual references reveals a strong ecclesiological undercurrent operating throughout all the various subdivisions of the text on the eucharist. The eucharist is the center of Christian worship (E1). The eucharist gives life to the body of Christ and to each of its members (E2). The eucharist is the Church's act of thanksgiving and, through the Church, the world's act of thanksgiving (E4). The eucharist is an ecclesial act of proclamation and intercession (E7, 8,23,25). Through the power of the Spirit, the eucharist brings the life of the new creation to the Church (E14,18). The eucharist symbolizes and realizes the fellowship which constitutes the body of Christ (E19). The eucharist is a celebration of and a call to service of men and women in the world (E24, 25). Unlike the preceding text on baptism, no major section of the text on eucharist lacks the ecclesiological referent.

Ecclesiological Dimensions of Baptism

Four essential ecclesiological elements are rightly underscored in the Lima document's treatment of baptism. First, baptism can only be comprehended within the corporate and liturgical life of the Church. Second, baptism is meaningful only in terms of personal faith. Third, baptism is the basis for the Christian responsibility of service for the Church and the world. Fourth, baptism is the foundation and constant challenge for full ecclesial communion among the churches.

The BEM text clearly identifies baptism as "intimately connected with the corporate life and worship of the Church" (B23). Likewise, the text notes the Church as the community of faith (B12) as the common element in believer baptism and the baptism of infants. Consequently, any satisfactory theological reflection on baptism must assume as its starting point an ecclesiological context. Failure to root baptism in the corporate structure of the Church will result in an inadequate and incomplete paradigm that is theologically distorted.

When baptism is intimately linked with the corporate life of the Church, one can more clearly comprehend how an individual is linked by baptism to Christ and how it is that baptism results in the remission of sin. [8] The Church is the historical presence of Christ in the world. By entering into a foundational relationship with the Church, an individual is necessarily related to Christ as the underlying power,

96

authority and person of this community. By entering
into a foundational relationship with the Church, an
individual moves from a world partially structured
toward sin to a community attempting to fully embrace
gospel values. This shift is a real _metanoia_ or
conversion. In short, the essential ecclesial character of baptism avoids the pitfalls of isolated individ-
ualism and magic and embraces a Christ-centeredness and
graced existence rooted in anthropological processes
and structures operating in concert with the gift of
faith.

To insist on the corporate-liturgical character of
baptism also heightens the baptismal action as a
corporate practice of the Church. The responsibility
for baptism lies not only in the minister of the one
being baptized, but especially in the whole people to
whom an individual is being joined. This vision
certainly remains faithful to the paradigmatic mode of
God's salvific activity in the Jewish and Christian
Scriptures. God saves us as individuals by forming us
into the community of His people. [9]

The symbolic actions of baptism are efficacious to
the extent that faith is operative in the candidate for
baptism. The Lima text presents this necessary character of faith as a "personal commitment" (B8). One
senses that the textual reference to a commitment
refers to responsible Christian activities of service
both for the Church and the world (B9). The call to
"personal faith," however, should not be conceived as
private. Individual faith is commensurately corporate
faith, the faith of the Church. The fact of baptism
should disclose a dual recognition. On the one hand,
the individual recognizes a reflection of his or her
deepest convictions in the ecclesial community which in
turn judges that the individual shares its corporate
comprehension of faith and a lifestyle demanded by it
to a satisfactory degree. Faith in action is the
clearest testimony to the efficaciousness of the
baptismal symbol.

The personal-corporate faith of baptism demonstrates itself in responsible membership. Lima is
forthright in identifying this responsibility as a
testimony to the Gospel in service of the Church and
the world (B9, 10). In no sense, then, is baptism a
sacred action which isolates individuals from the world
in order to construct a "salvation society" or a
"religious ghetto." All the baptized are intrinsically
called to turn toward the world as the audience for

their proclamation of the gospel and as the constituents of their service.

It is important to note that only in the performance of service is the full significance of baptism discovered. This suggests that baptism is not an isolated solitary action performed for an individual, but an unfolding life-long process that can be continually deepened and realized. Baptism challenges new members to be of service to the Church and the world (B10).

The present fragmentation and divisions within the Church weakens both the symbolic power of baptism as a sign of Christian unity and the effectiveness of service by the baptized to both the Church and the world. The Lima text positively notes that a theological vision of baptism is a call to embrace the ecumenical process and to seek the full visible unity of the Church. The common reality of baptism is already a manifestation of unity, but it is incomplete. The sacramental act of baptism is a testimony to ecclesial communion since all Christians share a common relationship to Christ and the Church of every age. Yet, the union symbolized in baptism is not a reality in our present age. In a real sense, then, sacramental meaning of baptism is constitutively related to ecclesiological reality and expressions.

Without denying the positive ecclesiological components present in the text on baptism, certain ecclesiological deficiences can equally be noted. First, there are tendencies in the text that suggest an excessively individualistic understanding of faith, grace and baptism. Second, the omission of an ecclesial dimension in the section on conversion, pardoning and cleansing can fail to underscore the process in which conversion and forgiveness actually transpire. Third, the omission of an ecclesial dimension in the section treating the gift of the Spirit fails to specifically identify the gift as a charism for the good of the Church and the world. Finally, one discovers a preponderant usage of the title body of Christ for the Church with a serious neglect of other ecclesial titles that yield a different ecclesiological perspective.

Although the Lima document insists that baptism unites the individual to the Church, this affirmation appears somewhat secondary to the union of the individual with Christ. The text suggests that our

ecclesial communion is based on our individual union
with Christ. This vision is not incorrect per se. One
might inquire, however, whether it would be more
accurate to envisage the union of the baptized with
Christ and the Church as a simultaneous and commensu-
rate happening. This interpretation would find expression in a statement affording an instrumentality to
the Church in terms of the union of the baptized with
Christ (i.e., baptism joins us to Christ through the
Church). Certain advantages would appear within this
perspective. First, the proposed shift would underscore the theological relationship of christology and
ecclesiology and affirm the role of the Church as the
historical presence in the world. Second, the shift
would enable a more facile understanding of the
anthropological substructures at work in the process of
faith and baptism--substructures which are corporate
and social in nature. Third, the shift would clearly
affirm the life of the Church as the ground of
sacramental praxis. Finally, the shift would inhibit
any "privatizing" or "spiritualizing" of faith by
insisting on its ecclesial character. [10]

Although the Lima text affirms the forgiveness of
sins by Christ through baptism and the assumption of a
new ethical orientation guided by the Holy Spirit, it
omits any reference to the Church in articulating these
phenomena. This omission tends to reinforce the
suspicion of a tendency toward an individualistic and
privatized portrayal of faith and baptism. Moreover,
it raises questions about the unthematized meaning of
sin behind the text.

Recent ethical reflections on sin have stressed
its social nature. [11] All sin disrupts the social
fabric and existence and therefore impinges on the
community of humankind. Theological writings on
reconciliation and conversion have consequently insist-
ed on their corporate and communal structures. [12] It
is in and through the action of the community of faith
that Christ forgives sin and that the Spirit guides the
conversion process. The sacramental action of baptism
does not operate differently from the eucharist or the
sacrament of reconciliation in this regard. Perhaps
the issue becomes clear through the example of contemporary theological analysis of original sin, its
transmission and its forgiveness in baptism. The term
original sin seeks to describe the situation or condition of non-salvation. [13] This condition arises from
being born into a world whose social structures orient
people away from gospel values and toward egoism.

99

Baptism alters this situation precisely by changing the community in which one grows and lives. Incorporation into the Church is an entry into structure and values of the gospel. This is the basic "stuff" of conversion.

The above perspective finds additional support in contemporary theological writings on the meaning of the res et sacramentum in sacramental theology. [14] Rather than viewing the sacramental rite (sacramentum tantum) as creating a character or adornment of the soul prior to and entering into the causality of grace (res tantum), contemporary authors see the sacramental rite as establishing a relationship to or status within the Church. Before God bestows his love on an individual, he makes one more deeply a part of his people which is his primordial act of saving love.

The Lima document affords a role to the Spirit in its exposition of baptism. The Spirit is at work before, during and after baptism. The Spirit guides the individual's life in a new ethical perspective. It is unfortunate again that here the text contains no explicit ecclesiological reference. This situation could be easily rectified by understanding the gift of the Spirit as a charism. The bestowal of the Spirit not only benefits the individual Christian, but is also a gift destined for the building up of the Church and the world. A more explicit ecclesiological perspective in the section on baptism and the gift of the Spirit would enhance Lima's proper insistence that baptism expresses itself in service.

The final ecclesiological criticism of the baptism text concerns the title utilized for the Church. Lima almost exclusively refers to the Church as the body of Christ. This decision may be judged short-sighted in view of the limitations implicit in the use of this title vis-a-vis others. The title body of Christ too easily suggests that the Church is a perfect community as Christ is perfect. It suggests a Church that is hierarchical in structure and static in nature. It suggests that the Church is coextensive to and identical with the risen Christ. Although these suggestions may not completely portray the meaning of the title as witnessed in the Pauline corpus, they are easily found in the pre-Vatican II magisterial teaching and theological writings on the Church. One of the great ecclesiological recoveries of the theological community and Vatican II was the use of the title People of God. This title suggest a Church of equality before differentiations of function and authority. It suggests a Church on pilgrimage, a dynamic community continually reforming itself as it moves through history toward the kingdom of God. [15]

In summary, an ecclesiological evaluation of the baptism text demonstrates both strengths and weaknesses. On the one hand, the Lima document seriously affirms the Church as the locus for understanding baptism and highlights the corporate responsibility for service which flows from baptism. On the other hand, its perspective fails to apply the ecclesial principle consistently in all the various dimensions of baptism which it chooses to address.

Ecclesiological Dimensions of the Eucharist

The Lima document arranges its presentation of the eucharist according to certain themes which have generally been utilized to articulate the multiple dimensions of eucharistic faith. The presence of an ecclesiological consciousness is felt throughout the text. Every subdivision contains ecclesiological references. In unfolding the eucharist as worship, thanksgiving-memorial, pneumatological communion and eschatological sign, the text accentuates an ecclesiology which is constitutive, central and service oriented.

The eucharist is the Church's central act of worship (E1). Eucharistic participation is a corporate action, a community celebration concretely symbolized in the eating of bread and drinking of wine (E2) in faithfulness to the Lord's command. The symbolic action of the eucharist realizes a communion with Christ and new life for His body in the forgiveness of sins and the promise of eternal life. Only the corporate body of the Church can celebrate the eucharist. It can never be correctly comprehended as a private or individual action. The Church's eucharistic celebration is a thanksgiving to the Father for creation and salvation. In this affirmation, the text is situating ecclesiology cosmically and historically. The Church is cast in a representative role. It speaks on behalf of all creation of which it is itself a part (E4).

The Church's eucharist is a memorial proclamation (E7) which challenges the Church to remember its origins, realize them in the present time and look forward to their fullness in the ages to come. The fact of the eucharist being celebrated by and within the Church is the most vivid testimony that the community of faith is witnessing to its heritage and fulfilling its responsibility of proclaiming God's mighty act of salvation to all the nations. The eucharist, therefore, is an ecclesial continuation of the ministry of Jesus in the world.

The Church does not attempt to celebrate the eucharist by drawing exclusively on human memory, good will or erudite planning. The eucharist is a pneumatological event effective only under the power, guidance and presence of Holy Spirit. The Spirit who makes the eucharistic event a reality (E14) is the same Spirit who forms and guides the whole life of the ecclesial community. The Holy Spirit links the Church to Christ and at the same time offers a foretaste of the kingdom of God (E18).

The Lima text clearly identifies the eucharist as the sign and cause of ecclesial communion (E19). The eucharistic celebration is the high point and full manifestation of ecclesial union. This ecclesial communion is both "transhistorical" and "cosmic." The eucharist is always a local celebration by a particular group of Christians. The unity presumed and effected in and through the celebration extends beyond the local church in its sociological and geographical identity to eucharistic celebrations of all times and places. The whole Church is involved in each local celebration of the eucharist. The eucharist, therefore, is never a private liturgical act of either an individual or a local community. Its ecclesial nature extends beyond the person and particular church to the Church through-out the ages and the world.

In identifying the relationship between eucharist and the kingdom of God, the text presents the Church as offering thanksgiving for the renewal already achieved and anticipating the full arrival of the kingdom. It identifies in an insightful way the presence of the world within the eucharistic celebration, for it is the world which will be the recipient of the blessings of the kingdom of God. The Church is the medium for both the world's presence in the eucharistic celebration and the renewal of the world in the Kingdom of God (E23). Ghettoized or isolationist ecclesiologies are foreign to eucharistic celebrations. The prime focus of the kingdom is not the Church, but the world. This principle must be incorporated into ecclesiology and therefore into eucharistic theology and practice. A service-oriented relationship between the Church and the world is rooted in this ecclesial-eucharistic vision. Those who celebrate the eucharist are to be servants of reconciliation among all people (E24). The eucharist is the ecclesial celebration of Christ's service and an ecclesial call to continue this service to the world. The Church continues Jesus' ministry of service in history through its social actions for the betterment of humankind. The Church must act as the eucharist which it celebrates and proclaims.

In contrast to the document on baptism, the text's treatment of the eucharist reveals few, if any, shortcomings from an ecclesiological perspective. One does detect a similar propensity in the text for selecting the title body of Christ for the Church. In view of the eucharistic context this is not surprising nor as much a deficiency as in the case of baptism. Still one might wish to see the perfectionist tendency of this title modified by some explicit recognition that the Church is in the process of fully conforming itself to being the body of Christ.

The ecclesiological underpinnings of the eucharistic text allow the Lima text to make theological advances in its eucharistic vision. First, the insistence on the eucharist as an action of the Church which invokes the power and presence of the Spirit permits the document to affirm the real presence of Christ in the eucharistic celebration. Second, the text properly demonstrates that Church life and eucharistic praxis ultimately point to service. In effect, the eucharist is the highpoint of ecclesial service. Third, the document boldly asserts that the world is the focus of ecclesial service and therefore, through the Church, intimately a part of eucharistic action. The ecclesiology operative in Lima's eucharistic text is more than adequate. The text unfolds not only the faith of the Church throughout the ages, but also many of the insights of the contemporary age which seek to clarify and apply the faith tradition of the Church to our present needs and longings.

BEM and RCIA

Any evaluation of BEM's reception by the Church as a statement of faith requires a comparison of the document with the various traditions now operative within different ecclesial communions. For Roman Catholicism, this task is lightened since the publication of the documents of Vatican II and the revision of

103

liturgical rites since the Council. By comparing the
Lima document and the Rite of Christian Initiation of
Adults (RCIA), the question of BEM's possible reception
by Roman Catholics becomes more clearly focused.

The Rite of Christian Initiation of Adults,
promulgated in 1972, was one of the major liturgical
reforms stemming from the Vatican II. As the official
rite of adult initiation, it represents an essential
datum in any formulation of a baptism theology. The
rite includes a general outline of the stages and
process of initiation, an examination of various roles
and the actual liturgical forms and prayers throughout
the initiation process.

The RCIA reflects an ecclesiology quite different
from one normally discovered in Roman Catholic teaching
and theological writings before the Council. [16]
First, initiation is presented as a process. Second,
the whole ecclesial communion bears responsibility for
the task of initiating new members into the community.
Third, there are multiple ecclesial ministries operative in the community so that this process might be
successful and the candidates for membership might be
afforded the full attention and service of the community on their journey to full membership in the Church.

The RCIA repeatedly stresses the responsibility of
the whole community in the whole initiation process.
No. 4 states that initiation takes place "in the midst
of the community of the faithful" who are themselves
intimately involved in reflecting "upon the value of
the paschal mystery, renew their own conversion, and by
their example lead the catechumens to obey the Holy
Spirit more generously."

In Section A: Evangelization and Precatechumenate,
no. 11 remarks that the whole Church elucidates the
gospel: "During this time, catechists, deacons, and
priests, as well as laypersons, suitably explain the
Gospel to the candidates." In Section B:
Catechumenate, no. 16 places responsibility to judge
the external indications of the catechumen not on the
priest alone, but with all who are involved in the
initiation process. Likewise, no. 19 places the
responsibility for the intellectual formation of the
catechumen on a variety of persons: "A fitting formation by priests, deacons, or catechists and other
laypersons given in stages and presented integrally ...
leads the catechumens to a suitable knowledge of dogmas
and precepts and also to an intimate understanding of

the mystery of salvation in which they desire to share. In the practical way of Christian life, the catechumen is helped and supported by sponsors and godparents and the whole community." The clearest statement of the ecclesial responsibility for initiation is in no. 41:

> Besides what is explained in the General Introduction, the people of God, represented by the local church, should always understand and show that the initiation of adults is its concern and the business of all the baptized. Therefore the community must always be ready to fulfill its apostolic vocation by giving help to those who need Christ. In the various circumstances of daily life, as in the apostolate, each disciple of Christ has the obligation of spreading the faith according to his capacity. Hence, the community must help candidates and the catechumens throughout their whole period of initiation, during the precatechumenate, the catechumenate, and the period of the postbaptismal catechesis or mystagogia.

Note should be taken of the specific language utilized in the text. First, people of God is correlated with the local church. Second, this local church should always understand and demonstrate that the initiation of adults is the concern of all the baptized. Third, the concern is identified with the Church's apostolic vocation of forming Christians. Finally, each Christian within the community shares in this responsibility.

The process of initiation outlined on the RCIA requires a variety and richness of ministries to bring about its actual fruition. The richness of ecclesiology found in the description of the initiation process finds equal expression in the presentation of the various ministries linked to initiation. The document identifies the ministries of catechist, sponsor, deacon, priest and bishop. The RCIA presents grass roots, emphasizing the communal structure of the Church and recognizing the variety of gifts within the local ekklēsia. This is an ecclesiology of involvement and witness, an ecclesiology which invites and elicits participation from below and within, rather that from without and above. This is an ecclesiology where theory is wedded to praxis, a community and

105

Church based on both sociability (rules) and comradeship (koinōnia). [17]

When the ecclesiology operating behind BEM and RCIA are compared, one sees both similarities and differences. Both documents clearly insist that the locus and context for an adequate comprehension of baptism is the community of faith. Both documents underscore the necessity of authentic conversion and personal faith as prerequisites for the sacramental celebration of initiation. There is no surprise, therefore, in discovering that both the BEM and RCIA stress the avoidance of indiscriminate baptismal practices. This reflects authentic pastoral care not only for the individual candidate but, more importantly, for the ecclesial communion itself.

The differences between the ecclesiology of RCIA and BEM might best be characterized as levels of emphasis and clarity. One discovers in RCIA a specific "structure" to the initiation process which points out the ecclesial nature of the process. Although BEM notes the developmental nature of initiation, no description or presentation of this process is given. Whereas RCIA identifies the ecclesial components and operations within the sacramental rites of the catechumenate (baptism, confirmation and eucharist), BEM requires its readers to draw out (or perhaps to read in) the ecclesiological dimensions of these sacramental processes. It appears that BEM lacks the specific and formal link of ecclesiology and sacramentology found in the contemporary Roman Catholic tradition.

Conclusion

It would be premature at the current juncture to judge whether or not the Lima document will be received by the churches as a statement of faith throughout the ages. If this reception is to become a reality, however, the document will undergo extensive evaluation and weighing by many parts of the Church. In this essay I have attempted a narrowly defined element of this exploration from a Roman Catholic perspective, i.e., exploring the implicit ecclesiology behind its statements on baptism and eucharist.

In examining the ecclesiology of BEM both strengths and deficiencies have been discovered. These do not require repetition. There is, however, one major difficulty which is helpful to note by way of

106

conclusion. Perhaps the greatest difficulty in responding to the text "as is" (and this is clearly
requested in the introduction) is the absence of any
official commentary which might assist in comprehending
the intention of the text and arriving at a correct
interpretation of the text. Baptism, Eucharist and
Ministry clearly addresses aspects of ecclesial life
which have traditionally been known as sacraments.
Yet, one fails to discover in the text an exposition of
a theology of the Church or sacraments which would
enable the reader to comprehend more accurately the
assertions of the document. [18]

The omission of such an exposition within the text
or in an accompanying commentary places an enormous
burden on the reader who must continually guess what
exactly the text is saying. One example may suffice
cited from E15 that states:

> It is in virtue of the living word of
> Christ and by the power of the Holy Spirit
> that the bread and wine become the
> sacramental signs of Christ's body and blood.
> They remain so for the purpose of communion.

If the term "sacramental sign" bears the same meaning
as found in the Roman Catholic tradition, this text
agrees with the Roman Catholic teaching concerning the
real presence of Christ in the eucharist. If the term
"sacramental sign" is taken in a different sense, e.g.
a Calvinistic sense, it might not reflect Roman Catholic conviction. Nowhere, however, is the meaning of
the term clearly delineated.

In the final analysis, BEM is a statement of how
far the ecclesial journey to unity has traversed and an
indication of how far the churches still need to walk
together before reaching full communion. Studying the
ecclesiology behind the text will help make that
journey one of hope and realism.

Notes for Chapter VII

1. <u>Baptism, Eucharist and Ministry</u> (Faith and Order Paper 111; Geneva: WCC, 1982) VII-X.

2. BEM, Preface, p. X.

3. BEM, Preface, p. IX.

4. <u>Ordo Initiationis Christianae Adultorum</u> (Rome: Vatican Press, 1972). English translation in <u>Document on the Liturgy, 1963-1979: Conciliar, Papal, and Curial Texts</u>, ed. ICEL (Collegeville: Liturgical, 1982) 736-61.

5. See: E. Schillebeeckx, <u>Christ the Sacrament of Encounter with God</u> (New York: Sheed and Ward, 1963); K. Rahner, <u>The Church and Sacraments</u> (New York: Herder and Herder, 1962); O. Semmelroth, "The Integral Idea of the Church," in <u>Theology Today</u>, Vol. 1 (Milwaukee: Bruce, 1965).

6. See: E. Kilmartin, "A Modern Approach to the Word of God and Sacraments of Christ: Perspectives and Principles," in <u>Sacraments: God's Love and Mercy Actualized</u> (Villanova: University of Villanova Press, 1979) 59-101.

7. See: G. Worgul, <u>From Magic to Metaphor</u> (New York: Paulist, 1980) 135-40.

8. Ibid. 145-51, 162-63.

9. See: G. Von Rad, <u>The Message of the Prophets</u> (London: SCM Press, 1968) 77-99; and G. Worgul, "Romans 9-11 and Ecclesiology," <u>Biblical Theology Bulletin</u> 12 (1982) 99-109.

10. See: A. Brunner, "Faith and Community," in <u>Toward a Theology of Christian Faith</u> (New York: Kennedy, 1968) 245-60.

11. See: P. Schoonenberg, <u>Man and Sin</u> (Notre Dame: University of Notre Dame Press, 1965); D. Kelly, "Aspects of Sin in Today's Theology," <u>Louvain Studies</u> 9 (1982) 191-97; "The Need for Salvation Symposium," <u>Chicago Studies</u> 21 (1982) 211-306; P. McVerry, "Sin: The Social, National and International Aspects," <u>The Way, Supplement</u> 48 (1983) 39-49.

12. See: P. Anciaux, "The Ecclesial Dimensions of Penance," in The Mystery of Sin and Forgiveness (New York: Alba House, 1971) 155-65; K. Rahner, "Forgotten Truths Concerning the Sacrament of Penance," in Theological Investigations, Vol. 2 (Baltimore: Helicon, 1963) 135-75.

13. Z. Alszeghy and M. Flick, "Il peccato originale in prospectiva personalistica," Gregorianum 46 (1965) 705-32.

14. See: T. Miyakawa, "The Ecclesial Meaning of the 'Res et Sacramentum'," The Thomist 31 (1967) 386ff.; R. King, "The Origin and Meaning of a Sacramental Formula: Sacramentum Tantum, Res et Sacramentum, Res Tantum," The Thomist 31 (1967) 21-82; and G. Worgul, From Magic, 144-52.

15. For a comparison of the different ecclesiologies of the Pauline titles, see: G. Worgul, "People of God, Body of Christ: Pauline Ecclesiological Contrasts," Biblical Theology Bulletin 21 (1982) 24-28.

16. G. Worgul, "The Ecclesiology of the Rite of Christian Initiation of Adults," Louvain Studies 6 (1976) 159-69.

17. Ibid. 168.

18. J. Coventry, "Baptism-Eucharist-Ministry: A Roman Catholic Response," One in Christ 20 (1984) 2-4.

CHAPTER VIII:

FAITH AND BAPTISM:
SACRAMENTAL THEOLOGY IN THE LIMA DOCUMENT

Edward J. Kilmartin, S.J.

FAITH AND BAPTISM:
SACRAMENTAL THEOLOGY IN THE LIMA DOCUMENT

Edward J. Kilmartin, S.J.

The Lima text presupposes that the fundamental structure of justification-sanctification is the same despite the various historical modes of its mediation. Whether it be verbal preaching of the word of God or the traditional sacraments of Christ, the offer of saving grace reaches its term through a response of faith. While a precise analysis of the relation between faith and sacraments is not provided, a concrete application of the theology of justification by faith is given attention in the text on baptism. For infant baptism is rejected by some churches of the so-called radical Reform movement.

The references to faith and eucharist in BEM also appear to be motivated by an ecumenical concern. They point to the intimate link between baptism and eucharist. Consequently, a challenge is placed before the churches to work out together a more profound understanding of the relationship between these two sacraments which might, for example, issue in common norms for the frequency of celebration of the Lord's Supper. However, there is an ecumenical problem associated with the interpretation of the liturgical prayer which follows the recitation of the account of institution of the eucharist in the Roman canon and Byzantine anaphoras. This prayer, which manifests the Church's intention to offer Christ's sacrifice to the Father, was categorically rejected by the classical Reformers as superstitious, calculated to weaken the cardinal principle of justification by faith alone. BEM does not refer to this issue, although it remains a theological problem in search of an ecumenical solution.

The subject of this essay is the relationship between faith and sacraments as expressed in the Lima text. Since this topic is developed at greater length in the text on baptism, an analysis of the genesis, content and critique of its teaching is given. BEM's teaching about the formal relation of faith to the eucharist requires no extended treatment. But its omission of some discussion of the anamnēsis prayer of offering causes some uneasiness from the standpoint of the Roman Catholic liturgical tradition. In the light of the continued opposition to this prayer within some Reformation circles, a brief comment on its profound

113

theological significance, precisely in relation to the theology of justification by faith, seems appropriate.

I.   Baptism and Faith in the Lima Text

The statement on baptism represents the fruit of many years of work of the Faith and Order Commission. [1] Key stages of the evolution of the text are record-ed in three previously published reports: The Meaning of Baptism [2]; Baptism, Confirmation and Eucharist [3]; One Baptism, One Eucharist and a Mutually Recognized Ministry. [4] A review of the content of these docu-ments furnishes background for a better understanding and evaluation of Lima on the subject of baptism and faith. In this essay they are referred to as One Lord, Louvain, and Accra.

1. Baptism and Faith in the Text One Lord. The report on The Meaning of Baptism in One Lord poses the question: Should only those be baptized who can make a "personal profession of faith?" [5] A partial answer is given in section III.2: The Relation of Faith to Baptism, [6] which furnishes the theological basis for subsequent expositions of the theme in Faith and Order documents.

Faith is described as necessary for the acquisition of the salvation promised to the faith. As associated with baptism, it is not simply a belief in the efficacy of baptism. Rather it is a "total response to the gift of God in Christ." [7] Grounded on God's work, faith is "the point of intersection of the sovereign work of God and the responsible action of man." [8] Scripture takes account of both the reality of the human response and the divine action, while stressing the priority of the latter by situating faith in relation to the divine election. According to One Lord, the paradox, charac-teristic of all attempts to describe the relation between divine sovereignty and human freedom, is espe-cially represented in the teaching that faith is a gift of the Spirit and "the Spirit is gained by the faith." [9]

These remarks on the relation of faith to grace are followed by an analysis of that between faith and baptism. At the outset a structural correspondence is affirmed between the event in which the adult comes to faith by hearing the word of God and the event of adult baptism. In both cases the decision of the person presupposes and proclaims the election by God. This serves as an introduction to a comparison between adult

114

and infant baptism in which the tertium comparationis is the divine election and ecclesial context.

The theological grounds for the exclusive practice of believers' baptism is contrasted with that used to support infant baptism. Believer baptist churches view baptism as "the crowning moment and goal of the faith which turns to the Lord." As a consequence of this unilateral understanding, "the presence of personal faith in the recipient of baptism is considered essential." However, One Lord recalls that the explicit decision of the adult who seeks baptism is based on the previous decision of the Trinity. Moreover, the adult decision "has its setting within the life and faith of the Church and though the life and witness of the whole Church declares the faithfulness of God, the ground of all decisions of faith." [10]

This pericope, incorporated into Accra V.12, emphasizes the divine initiative, the subjective participation of the adult subject of baptism in the faith of the Church and the ecclesial setting of baptism. The description of infant baptism, repeated in Accra V.13, highlights the first and third aspects and also stresses the commitment of the community to support the infant's growth in the life of faith.

> The practice of infant baptism occurs in
> the context in which stress is laid upon
> the corporate faith, upon the environment
> of faith, rather than upon the explicit
> decision of the recipient of baptism.
> Here the whole community affirms its
> faith in God and pledges itself to provide
> such an environment of faith, in the house
> and in worship, instruction and witness of
> the Church. [11]

Also a correspondence is established between the subjective commitment of the adult who seeks baptism and that of the person baptized in infancy. The passage, repeated in Accra V.14, refers to the need for subsequent personal engagement in faith on the part of the one baptized in infancy.

> The necessity of the baptized himself to
> believe is not diminished in any way, far
> less removed. The claim and promise of the
> Gospel are laid on the child in baptism
> to which a response of obedience must be
> owed and which must be received by faith,

115

if the fruits of baptism are to be known
and to flourish in his life. [12]

Finally the decision to have the infant baptized, just
as the personal decision of the adult who seeks baptism,
is situated in the prior decision of God. The "decision
of God, his fidelity to his promises, the gift which he
makes in the baptism of Jesus Christ" accounts for the
"environment of faith" in which the infant is placed.
The decision to baptize the child "just as the personal
decision of the believer who is baptized, is itself a
means for the proclamation of God's own faithfulness."
[13]

In summary, several conclusions may be drawn. One
Lord takes for granted the sacramental nature of
baptism. This viewpoint is already expressed in its
first section: The Divine Trinity and the Unity of the
Church VII: The Church, Worship and Sacraments. Those
who question whether both preaching and sacraments are
normally necessary for salvation are not in harmony with
the traditional teaching and practice of the Church.
[14] Louvain also asks how certain post-Reformation
movements, which either reject the use of exterior
sacramental signs or show a relatively weak interest in
them, can reconcile their attitude with the New Testament. [15]

Both One Lord and Louvain assign to baptism a
christological origin and consider it to have held a
central place in the Church's life from an early date.
This point of view is also expressed in Accra I.1, where
sacraments are described as "Christ's gift to his
Church," as well as in Lima I.1's qualification of
baptism as "a gift of God."

Throughout the reports we are considering, a
consistent position is taken on the sacramental
character of baptism. It is not a dispensable addition
to the preaching of the word of God. Rather it is a
ritual form of the offer of salvation, willed by God as
a means of incorporation into the Church.

Furthermore, according to One Lord both baptized
believers and infants participate in one baptism. Both
participate in the faith of the Church, ritually
expressed in the rite and personally present in the
gathered community. The infant participates through the
decision of those who present it for baptism; the adult
candidate subjectively participates through a personal
confession of the faith of the Church. The decision for

116

baptism in both cases is grounded on the divine initiative.

Two ambiguities remain concerning One Lord's teaching about faith and infant baptism. One has to do with the efficacy of infant baptism and the other with the relationship of the infant to the act of faith of those who present it for baptism.

First, One Lord remarks that in baptism "the claim and promise of the Gospel are laid on the infant" (III. 2). This description of the real effects of infant baptism is rather vague. The language recalls Calvin's theology of infant baptism, where the promise of the covenant is efficacious for the infant from the mother's womb in the case of believing parents and the present efficacy of infant baptism relates more to the strengthening of the faith of the parents and community in God's promise. Still the citation occurs in a context which refers to the necessity of a personal response of faith by the one baptized in infancy if "the fruits of his baptism" are to flourish. Moreover, One Lord knows only one baptism. Hence, it can be supposed that the meaning of this one baptism, described elsewhere, [16] is equally applicable to both forms of baptism.

Secondly, One Lord does not provide a full explanation of the role of the faith of the Church in infant baptism. Since it is explained in various ways in the history of theology, some attention should be given to this problem. Does the faith of the Church play a different role, an essentially different role, in infant baptism than it plays in adult baptism? What is the function of "vicarious faith" (fides aliena) in infant baptism? Does it merely enter on the side of the realization of the sacramental symbolic action, as word which interprets the sacramental gesture? Is it more than a pledge of active responsibility for the religious development of the infant? Is it also a form of intercession for the salvation of the infant in the sense that the infant can be said to be sanctified by the intercessory prayer of the Church? Does the fides aliena really substitute for the personal subjective response of faith of the infant so that the infant can be said to receive sanctification in the measure of the community's openness to grace in favor of the infant?

2. Baptism and Faith in the Louvain Text. The Louvain document situates the theme of baptism and faith within the broader context of the unity of baptism. [17] Three

aspects of the unity of baptism are identified. Baptism is a unique act which cannot be repeated. According to many traditions there is simply one baptism, identical in the case of infant and believers' baptism. Finally, the one baptism is the "clearest sign of unity ... which still exists between the churches." [18] Therefore churches which rebaptize those who received baptism in infancy not only call into question the identity between adult and infant baptism but also compromise the sign value of baptism as expression of the unity of the churches.

The divergent interpretations of the will of the Lord regarding the practice of baptism, which sometimes results in rebaptism, surface especially between believer baptist and paedobaptist churches. Hence Louvain concludes that the question of the faith of the candidate for baptism constitutes the core of the ecumenical problem. However the judgment is made that it should be possible for the churches to recognize each other's baptism as the one baptism "when Jesus Christ has been confessed as Lord by the candidate, or, in the case of infant baptism, by the Church on his behalf and when baptism had been performed with water in the name of the Father and the Son and the Holy Spirit." [19]

This solution, repeated in Accra VI.23 with an important additional qualification, [20] is supported by a comparison of the relation of faith to adult and infant baptism.

> In the case of believing adults the baptized
> person can make his own personal confession
> of faith and commitment. The baptism of the
> infant looks forward to this personal
> confession of faith and commitment. Thus the
> identity of adult believers' baptism and
> infant baptism can only be evident if the
> churches insist on the necessity of the
> vicarious faith of the congregation as well
> of the parents and sponsors. [21]

In this passage the lack of subjective faith in the infant is seen not to effect the unity of the one baptism. Reference is also made to the necessity of vicarious faith which makes evident the identity of adult and infant baptism. How is this "necessity" to be interpreted?

The act of faith of the community is said to include "the belief that participation in the corporate life of the body of Christ is an essential element in the salvation of each member and that the baptized infant is initiated into this corporate life." [22] Therefore the conclusion is drawn that "Indiscriminate infant baptism is irresponsible and turns infant baptism into an act which can hardly be understood to be essentially the same as adult believers' baptism." [23]

This language does not allow us to conclude that, according to Louvain, the identity of believers' and infant baptism, at the level of the real effects of infant baptism, depends on the existence of vicarious faith in the adults who actually present the infant and who otherwise are physically present at the rite. It seems clear that the necessity of vicarious faith is understood to be a relative necessity. With respect to the real effects of infant baptism, its absence does not stand in the way of the true administration of the sacrament. Louvain can hardly be supposed to take a stand against the position - which has a long history - that a person without faith can act as minister of baptism as long as he or she intends "to do what the Church does." On the other hand this same tradition is not insensitive to the ecclesiastical side of the sacrament. It recognizes that the presence of vicarious faith plays a significant role, or can play such a role, in the integration of the infant into the life of faith of the community. For it commits the community to responsible action in favor of the infant, corresponding to the ecclesial finality of baptism: incorporation into the the Church. In its concluding remarks Louvain refers to this "seriousness of the faith of those who bring children for baptism and on the necessity of ensuring that the child shall grow into the maturity of responsible faith." [24]

In the Louvain text, the theology of faith and baptism, faith and infant baptism, corresponds to that of One Lord. Also, as in One Lord, a solution to the problem of infant baptism vis-à-vis believers' baptism is sought with a view to responding to a concrete difficulty which threatens, in practice, the unicity of baptism and so the value of baptism as an expression of the unity of the churches. Louvain's comments on the theme of unity of baptism serves as a basis fo Accra VI.22.

3. Baptism and Faith in the Accra Text. Accra's One Baptism II.3,B refers to the connection between baptismal grace and faith. It is "received by those who believe in Jesus Christ." The opening sentence of II.

4,C is more explicit: "The necessity of faith for the reception of the salvation embodied and set forth in baptism is acknowledged by all churches." But, as the rest of pericope indicates, the weight of attention is focused on the role of faith in the acceptance of the baptismal grace throughout the whole of Christian life: "personal commitment ... to life-long growth of participation in Christ." The function of faith in the sacramental reception of the baptismal grace requires some elaboration in view of the practice of infant baptism. This is provided in Accra V. Different Approaches to Baptism of Infants and Believers (12-14).

Accra V.12-14, dependent on One Lord III.2, as well as Accra VI.22 which paraphrases Louvain VI, requires no special comment. However, the qualification added in Accra VI.23, which otherwise incorporates Louvain VI.A, on the subject of mutual recognition by the churches of one another's baptism, is noteworthy. The original formulation corresponds to the traditional position of paedobaptist churches. The new qualification: "and confirmed subsequently by personal commitment to Christ," seems to be inspired by recent concessions of some believer baptist congregations to receive as members those baptized in infancy without repeating baptism. But this qualification cannot be predicated of many traditional paedobaptist churches who, following the Augustinian tradition, recognize that grace is bound to the sacrament administered in the name of the Trinity with the intention "to do what the Church does." According to them the infant becomes, in mysterio, a believer in accord with the measure of its human development.

Accra VI.23 seems to imply that there are two distinct norms of recognition of infant baptism: one based on the confirmation of the divine election of the person baptized in infancy which is furnished subsequently "by personal commitment to Christ"; the other simply on the correct administration of the rite of baptism. However, to the extent that believer baptist churches employ the norm set forth in Accra VI. 23, the question of the value of infant baptism as such remains unresolved. The approach of Accra recalls the scholastic theory of "reviviscence of sacraments" (reviviscentia sacramentorum) i.e., a valid sacrament, unfruitful because of an obstacle to grace, becomes fruitful when the obstacle is removed. Only here the obstacle is a subjective disposition of the adult. The Accra norm seems to imply that the obstacle is the lack of subjective faith on the part of the infant - a point of view which is unacceptable to many paedobaptist churches.

The concluding paragraph of Accra's One Baptism (IV.24) seems to be sensitive to this difficulty. It urges "believer baptist and paedobaptist churches" to overcome their differences and points to three values "in responsible infant baptism, namely the place it gives the child in God's providence for his Church, the primacy it gives to God's act in Christ through the Spirit, and its longstanding practice in responsible churches which seek to act under the guidance of the Spirit." This invitation to rethink the practice of infant baptism within a more global perception of the life of faith is repeated in Lima B16 which refers only to the theme of God's providence.

4. Baptism and Faith in the Lima Text. The Lima document on baptism explains the "Meaning of Baptism" (B2-7) by outlining New Testament teaching about the baptismal grace as a gift of God in Christ through the Spirit. The other aspect, the human response to that gift, is discussed in the following section "Baptism and Faith" (B8-10).

"Baptism is both God's gift and our human response to that gift" (B8). This opening sentence is linked to material borrowed from Accra II.4,C which views baptism as the beginning of growth in Christ. Lima (B9-10) expands on the last two sentences of Accra II.4,C which refer to the personal commitment in faith required of baptized Christians. But B8, which quotes Accra II.4,C,1 receives no immediate attention insofar as it relates to infant baptism. "The necessity of faith for the reception of the salvation embodied and set forth in baptism" (B8), in relation to the practice of infant baptism, is discussed in B11-16. Baptismal Practice: A. Baptism of Believers and Infants (B11-12).

After outlining the practice of believers' and infant baptism (B11), the Lima text then compares the two forms (B12). BEM integrates material from the previous three Faith and Order reports, but reworks it to show as clearly as possible the correspondences between the two forms of baptism:
   1) Both forms of baptism take place in an ecclesial context (B12).
   2) Personal faith commitment is an integral part of believers' baptism and a necessary consequence of infant baptism (B12; Louvain VI.B).

121

3)   Both the adult and infant are committed to growth in faith after baptism (BCom 12).

4)   "All baptism" is situated within the life of faith of the Church and, through the witness of the Church's faith, points to God as "ground of all life of faith" (B12). The source of this statement in One Lord III.2 and Accra V.12 refers only to the "personal decision" of the adult believer.

5)   "At every baptism the whole congregation reaffirms its faith in God and pledges itself to provide an environment of witness and service" (B12). The source of this statement in One Lord III.2 and Accra V.13 refers only to infant baptism.

The Commentary added to B12 summarizes the similarities between believers' and infant baptism. Both "embody God's own initiative in Christ and express a response of faith made within the believing community." This statement could serve as the minor premise of which the major would be B8. This conclusion would then follow: All churches should be able to acknowledge both forms of baptism.

For the rest the Commentary on B12 takes over the thought and language of Accra V.12-14 to explain the differences and correspondences between the two forms of baptism. "Corporate faith (Accra V.13,1) and the faith which the child shares with its parents" (BCom 12) comes to the foreground in infant baptism. Adult baptism "emphasizes the explicit confession of the person who responds to the grace of God in and through the community of faith and who seeks baptism" (BCom 12; Accra V.12,4; One Lord III.2). But both forms of baptism "require a similar and responsible attitude towards Christian nurture" (BCom 12). For "the personal faith of the recipient and faithful participation in the life of the Church are essential for the full fruit of baptism" (BCom 12; Accra V.14,2b). There is also a reference to the efficacy of infant baptism which repeats Accra V.14,2b (One Lord III.2): "Through baptism, the promise and claim of the Gospel are laid upon the child" (BCom 12).

Lima B15 includes Accra V.23. But whereas the Accra text says that "The full recognition ... should be possible," the Lima text observes that "Churches are increasingly recognizing one another's baptism as the one baptism into Christ when Jesus Christ has been confessed as Lord by the candidate or, in the case of infant baptism, when confession has been made by the church (parents, guardians, godparents and congregation) and affirmed later by personal faith and commitment" (B 15). Hence the Lima text refers more directly to the concrete reasons why some believer baptists might accept the baptism of individuals who were baptized in infancy. But this hardly constitutes acceptance of infant baptism by believer baptists in the sense it is accepted by many paedobaptist churches - a difficulty discussed previously in the commentary on Accra V.23.

Lima places in greater relief the ecclesiological aspect of all baptism and outlines with greater clarity the correspondence and differences between believers' and infant baptism. However, there is no essential change in the theological presentation of the relationship between faith and sacraments and faith and infant baptism which goes beyond that expressed in the previous three documents. Consequently the two ambiguities mentioned in the commentary on One Lord III.2 remain: what is the role of faith of the Church in the baptism of infants and what are the real effects of infant baptism?

II. Response to Lima's Presentation of Faith and Infant Baptism. In the context of the believer-baptist debate, Lima emphasizes the ecclesiological aspect of the rite of infant baptism: the role of the faith of the Church. It is reminiscent of Augustine's teaching on infant baptism which, in a different context, offers deep reflection on the role of the Church in the event of infant baptism. His analysis of this theme can serve as point of departure for the ongoing debate between believer baptist and paedobaptist churches. It affords a very precise explanation about the role of the Church and, as a consequence, an unambiguous position regarding the real effects of infant baptism. But to what extent can the Augustinian approach to faith and sacrament be received within a modern approach to faith and sacrament which characteristically begins by asking what the liturgy of the sacraments has to say for itself?

1. Faith and Infant Baptism According to Augustine. The Bishop of Hippo's explanation of the meaning of infant baptism assumes that the infant plays a passive role. Physically alive but spiritually unborn, the infant is in need of the grace of rebirth. In the process which leads to the bath of regeneration, and through which the infant becomes a believer, [25] the primary role is exercised by the Holy Spirit; supporting actors are the offerentes and, above all, mater ecclesia.

123

The offerentes, those who present the infant and profess faith in the Trinity in its name, represent the universa societas sanctorum atque fidelium. For it is the mater ecclesia who gives birth to the individual members of the body of Christ. [26] The offerentes are employed by mater ecclesia to present the child for baptism. [27] When they respond for the infant, confessing faith in the Trinity, mater ecclesia uses their tongues. [28] Since the activity of the offerentes represents that of mater ecclesia, always united to Christ in the Spirit, it penetrates to the invisible level and results in the bestowal of the baptismal grace. [29]

The profession of faith, an essential element of the baptismal rite, is both a condition and sign of the presence of faith in the baptized infant. It obtains its goal, i.e., realizes what it signifies, when it is integrated into the sacramental action. For, Augustine reasons, the subject is only born anew "of water and the Holy Spirit." [30] The infant is regenerated by water which signifies the grace, supplies the sacramental sign of grace, and by the Spirit working interiorly.

In the context of a concrete pastoral problem Augustine excludes the notion that the infant is sanctified in baptism by the prayer of intercession of the parents or offerentes. For the utility of the will of the offerentes is subordinate to baptism itself and so to the sanctifying presence of the Spirit: "The Spirit who regenerates is identical in the adults who present and in the infant presented and regenerated. It is by participation in this one Spirit that the will of the offerentes is useful to the infant." [31]

This last statement responds to a difficulty posed by Bishop Boniface. He asks whether it is correct to say that the infant is saved by the faith of the parents. The question was occasioned by the practice of some African Christians who had their children baptized in the Church and then attempted to secure their salvation by having sacrifices offered to idols. Boniface reasons that if the faith of the parents contributes to the salvation of the infant, their sacrilegious acts must destroy the effect of baptism. Augustine rejects the argument. For the salutary effect of baptism is assured by the intervention of the Spirit, present in the baptized and the parents or offerentes, provided the sacrament is accomplished.

According to Augustine, the efficacy of the sacrament is rooted in the faith under two aspects. The faith of the Church intervenes to confer on the sacrament a transcendent meaning. It makes baptism an efficacious rite. The act of the Church conditions the saving presence of Christ and the Spirit. It is a "ministerial cause" of sacramental grace. On the other hand, the faith of the candidate is the way of reception. Its proper action does not relate to the objective aspect of sacramental efficacy: the realization of the sacramental offer of grace, but to the subjective aspect: the utility of the sacrament.

These two actions of faith, one creative and the other receptive of sacramental efficacy, are ontologically linked and this explains their complementary roles. The faith of the individual participates in the faith of the Church. It is under this title that the faith of the subject of baptism intervenes in an active way to obtain grace. Its proper role is to extend in the subjective domain the objective salutary action of the faith of the Church. Since the response of subjective faith places the subject in conformity with the faith of the Church, it allows the subject to participate in the supernatural effects of the reception of the sacrament. [32]

The faith of the subject is a disposition for baptismal grace. It opens the subject to be receptive of the salvation acquired through the sacrament, i.e., allows for the interior expansion of the grace newly acquired through baptism. In the case of the infant, the primacy and efficacy of the divine intervention explains the elevation of the baptized to the status of the new creature, and this means believer. The expansion of this grace of regeneration occurs as one responds to the Gospel throughout the whole of life's pilgrimage.

2. <u>Baptism as Symbolical Reality of Faith</u>. To what extent can the Augustinian approach to infant baptism be "received" within a modern approach to the theology of sacraments which began with the symbolic actions themselves and views the reality symbolized as so connected with the symbolic actions that it can only be approached as reality in and through the symbolic action?

If one begins the analysis of the meaning of baptism with the rite of adult baptism itself, as rite of initiation into the Church, the significance of the role of the Church in the explanation of the efficacy of baptism comes to the foreground. One sees immediately that the rite is a ritual expression of the faith of the Church, even at the level of the so-called essential rite which has its basis in the primary expression of the faith of the Church, the New Testament. It expresses the belief of the Church that God is offering the grace of salvation which corresponds to the human and social situation which it signifies. In other words, the decision to join a new member to itself by the Church is signified by the rite and, in turn, this signifies for the eyes of faith incorporation into the mystery of the Church: incorporation into Christ through the gift of the Spirit.

Correspondingly the utility of the sacrament, as celebration of the faith of the Church, is related to all the gathered members of the Church. In the case of the eucharist, proleptic messianic banquet, this is obvious. But it also holds for other traditional sacramental celebrations which are especially directed to specific individuals. In these instances the rite expresses the agreement of the Church with the grace being offered to one of its members. Since the community gratefully receives this grace bestowed on the individual, it is made aware of its responsibility to foster that individual's growth in the life of faith. This grateful response makes the community aware that all grace is a gift of God and so opens it to receive a deepening of the life of faith. It also occasions the reception of that grace which deepens the bond of unity between itself and the individual subject for whom the sacrament is celebrated.

Since the sacrament is primarily an act of the gathered community, the individual shares in the measure of his or her participation in the faith of the Church. The utility of the sacrament for the adult subject depends on the degree with which one can argue with the concrete expression of the faith of the Church. The adult believer who seeks baptism comes to the liturgy with a personal faith commitment. Through the celebration, which expresses the faith of the Church, he or she is both offered the baptismal grace as grace and is given, at the same time, the grace to agree with it by gratefully acknowledging that it is given apart from personal merit.

To the extent that one agrees with the faith of the Church that grace is being offered as grace through the rite, he or she is made more fully subject of the sacrament of baptism. Hence God's grace, incarnated in the faith of the Church expressed in the rite, appears in the first place as granting the disposition of the subject of the sacrament to respond to God's offer of grace. The remote dispositions, which lead the adult to seek baptism, obtain a new quality through integration into the faith of the Church expressed in the rite.

But if the specific efficacy of the sacraments can be described as enabling the individual adult to become subject of the sacramental celebration through subjective participation in the faith of the Church rather than simply as willing object of the sacramental bestowal of sacramental grace, how can this be reconciled with infant baptism? Infants do not bring a personal faith commitment to baptism and so do not participate through subjective conscious faith made more receptive through the announcement within the rite of the bestowal of God's grace in their favor.

The rite of infant baptism expresses the conviction that the Father, in Christ, through the Spirit who works through the faith of the Church, relates self to this specific personal point of reference. This commitment of the Trinity does not depend on the response of the subject of baptism. It is relational: The Father submits self to this point of reference without depending on it. Accomplished in and through the sacrament of faith, it is a transcendental act by which the Father sends the Spirit through and with the Son. Hence the communication of God's self is immediate. The sacramental rite is only the symbolic expression of this, calculated to enable the subject and the whole community to be aware of and open to the grace being offered by a transcendental act.

While the infant is not able to appropriate this offer of God's self communication by a subjective act of free will under grace, this does not change the fact that baptism is relational: related to the act of God communicating self to the infant and not dependent on the subjective dispositions of the infant. This is the belief manifested in the rite of infant baptism. But what is the origin of this belief?

The problem of infant baptism is not a typically Reformation question. Irenaeus defends it against Gnosticism. Origen, Tertullian and Cyprian speak of it as opponents of the Montanists. The practice represents an anomaly within the sacramental practice of the Church and this is supported by the fact that traditionally the

127

form of adult baptism is employed. The theological grounds for the origin of the practice cannot be established with certainty, nor can it be said with certainty where it first took root. However, as a consequence of the practice various attenpts have been made to show how it is orthopraxis.

Infant baptism seems to have originated, in the second or possibly first century, with a global perception of the life of faith and was retained because it was experienced as a behavior which harmonized with the practice of faith. The attempts to justify infant baptism were made on the basis of pre-established principles and inspired by practical pastoral problems. Consequently, the theological interpretations are always historically conditioned by the aspect under which it is considered and the expertise of the theologian. Moreover, it should not be expected that a concrete practice of the faith can be completely explained on the basis of a single theological principle. The reason is quite simple: Orthopraxis, the doing of the faith, is not reducible to the practical application of an abstract truth. Rather it incarnates a global perception of the faith which can never be captured by a rational synthesis.

Augustine appeals to the faith of <u>mater ecclesia</u> in order to establish the presence of the profession of faith required by Christ as an essential aspect of the rite of initiation. But this answers only one specific issue related to infant baptism. The necessity of infant baptism was especially stressed at the end of the fourth century. The grounds were a questionable theology of original sin and its consequences for the infant dying without baptism. The Augustinian appeal to the faith of the Church has proved to be of enduring value, though not always explained according to his point of view. The theological basis for the necessity of infant baptism has not had the same fate. This is all the more interesting because the appeal to the theology of original sin and its consequences for the infant has been the most popular traditional basis for the practice of infant baptism.

The formulation of doctrines results from reflection on the practice of the faith which has proven to correspond to an experience which impregnates and structures the existence of believers. Doctrines are judged to be true to the extent that they can be inserted into the lived act of faith of a community. But they are not sufficient to provide a completely satisfactory answer to what is recognized as orthopraxis through a more original experience of the life of faith. In the end it must be admitted that the recognition of infant baptism as orthodox can only be achieved by the experience of faith, grounded on the practice of faith, that it expresses the will of God.

III. "Offering Christ" and Justification by Faith. Lima's Baptism relates baptism to the eucharist. Since baptism is "incorporation into the body of Christ," it "points by its very nature to the eucharistic sharing of Christ's body and blood" (BCom 14b). Here it is taught that the eucharist is a sacramental means of deepening the baptismal incorporation into Christ. In addition, the eucharist is described as a public liturgical rite in which the event of baptism is repeatedly reaffirmed: "Baptism needs to be constantly reaffirmed. The most obvious form of such reaffirmation is the celebration of the eucharist" (BCom 14c). The implied relation between faith and eucharist, found in the baptism document, is explicitly mentioned in the eucharist text: "Christian faith is deepened by the celebration of the Lord's Supper" (E 30).

In the Lima statement on eucharist the significance of the anamnēsis offering prayer in relation to the reception of the gift of Christ bestowed through the eucharist is treated at length. Here it suffices to note that this traditional prayer of offering Christ to the Father seems to have been understood originally as the acknowledgement that the gift, though bestowed, remains a gift on which the recipients are totally dependent. The thankful offering of the gift is the liturgical way of affirming this fact. It is a profound affirmation of the doctrine of justification by faith alone and contributes to fostering the self-offering of Christians: their spiritual openness to receive the meaning of their lives by the Father's self-communication through Christ in the Spirit.

If properly understood this rite of "offering Christ" becomes the high point of the ritual act of faith of the Church. It condenses in itself the meaning of the whole eucharistic prayer and the deepest meaning of baptism which Lima rightly describes as "God's gift." Furthermore it brings out the depth of meaning contained in the saying that "Baptism is both God's gift and our human response to that gift" (B8). The response to God's gift must be the recognition that it always remains a gift. This response is expressed liturgically in full measure, and without ambiguity, in the fourth

eucharistic prayer of the new Roman Missal of Paul VI:
"We offer you his body and blood, the acceptable sacrifice which brings salvation to the whole world."

Notes for Chapter VIII

1. Baptism, Eucharist and Ministry (Faith and Order Paper 111; Geneva: WCC, 1982).

2. One Lord, One Baptism (Faith and Order Paper 29; London: SCM, 1960: The Divine Trinity and the Unity of the Church (7-44); The Meaning of Baptism (45-71).

3. Louvain 1971: Study Reports and Documents (Faith and Order Paper 59; Geneva: WCC, 1971) 35-53. This report was submitted to the Faith and Order Commission at its meeting in Louvain, 1971.

4. Faith and Order Paper 73; Geneva: WCC, 1975. This report is a revision of an amended text made at the Faith and Order Commission's meeting in Accra, Ghana, 1974.

5. I: Introduction, p.48.

6. pp. 61-64.

7. p. 62.

8. Ibid.

9. Ibid.

10. p. 63.

11. Ibid.

12. Ibid.

13. p. 64.

14. VII a, p. 35.

15. I.2: The Present Practice of the Churches, p. 38.

16. II.5: The Baptism of the Individual, pp. 55-57; III. Theological Implications and Questions. 1: The Meaning of Participation, pp. 58-61.

17. VI. The Unity of Baptismal Initiation, pp. 45-46.

18. VI, p. 45.

19. VI.A: The General Problem of Mutual Recognition, p. 46.

20. " ... or in the case of the infant by the Church on his behalf and confirmed subsequently by personal commitment to Christ."

21. VI.B: Believers' and Infant Baptism, p. 47.

22. VI.B, p. 47.

23. Ibid.

24. Ibid.

25. De peccatorum meritis et remissione I.20,26 (CSEL 60,27).

26. Letter to Bishop Boniface, Ep.98.5 (CSEL 34, 526).

27. Sermo 176.2 (Pl 38,950).

28. Sermo 244.2 (Pl 38,1342).

29. De pecc. mer. et rem. I.26,29 (CSEL 60,38).

30. Ep. 98.2 (CSEL 34,521).

31. Ep. 98.2 (CSEL 34,522).

32. Louis Villette, Foi et sacrement I: Du nouveau Testament à Saint Augustin (Travaux de l'Institut Catholique de Paris 5; Paris: Bloud et Gay, 1959) 287-88.

CHAPTER IX:

THE LIMA TEXT ON EUCHARIST

Edward J. Kilmartin, S.J.

THE LIMA TEXT ON EUCHARIST

Edward J. Kilmartin, S.J.

At the level of a formulation of faith, the Lima document on the eucharist reflects the understanding of the eucharist expressed in the Roman Catholic liturgical and theological tradition. Naturally some additions are required to bring it into correspondence with the modern official Roman Catholic approach to the interpretation of the liturgical event, notably the role of the priest as representative of Christ and of the Church, and the moment of consecration of the bread and wine. This also holds true for the Roman Catholic official explanation of the change of the eucharistic elements at the ontological level. However, the official interpretation of the liturgical event and the nature of the change of the elements is being subjected to critical reflection within Roman Catholic theology itself. The official teaching does not certainly represent a modern consensus of Catholic theology but rather a consensus of post-Tridentine theologians.

In the first part of this analysis a summary of the Lima text is given on which the subsequent analysis is based. The critique attempts to make clear the extent to which the statement conforms to the whole Roman Catholic tradition and to show how particular concerns of modern Roman Catholic scholarship might be integrated into it.

PART I

The division of this part follows that of the agreed statement which treats, in turn, the origin, meaning and celebration of the eucharist. Unless otherwise indicated this summary is intended to para-phrase the essential content of the text.

I.   The Institution of the Eucharist (E1). The New Testament witnesses to the relationship between the meals of Jesus' public life, the Last Supper and the meals of the risen Lord with his disciples. All proclaim and enact, in their own way, the fellowship of the kingdom. The eucharist has this same characteristic. However, it is the meal of the Church, the new people of God, which originates from the whole Christ event. Consequently from the standpoint of salvation history it is the memorial of the whole of the saving work of Christ, prefigured in the Passover memorial of the Exodus event which established Israel as God's

135

people and the meal of the covenant of Mt. Sinai which sealed Israel's commitment to Yahweh. The form of the eucharist derives from the Last Supper. It is given to the Church by the Lord as a way of remembering him and encountering him through symbolic words and actions and so sharing in the new covenant with the Father grounded on Christ's self-offering as representative of humanity.

II. The Meaning of the Eucharist (E 2-26). The analysis of the meaning of the eucharist begins with what is ultimately signified by the liturgical action. The celebration of the Church is the efficacious sign of the active presence of Christ who grants communion with himself and of the active presence of the Holy Spirit who is bestowed by the Father in a purely transcendental act, i.e., emanating immediately from the divinity itself. The action of Christ corresponds to the purely divine act by which believers receive forgiveness of sins and deeper incorporation into the body of Christ (E2).

The remainder of this section analyzes the chief themes of the liturgical forms of the ancient eucharistic liturgies of the East and West and shows how they relate to the mystery dimension of the eucharist. Its content can be quickly summarized.

1) The eucharist is a sacrifice of thanksgiving and praise directed to the Father for all his benefits. Spoken by the eucharistic assembly in the name of all creation, it is accompanied by intercession of the participants for themselves and all people. This sacrificial prayer is acceptable because Christ the High Priest unites the faithful of his Church to himself and includes their prayers in his intercession. As such the eucharist anticipates the day when all people will be united in the body of Christ, living in full communion with the Father and one another in the Holy Spirit (E3-4).

2) The eucharist is memorial of Christ. In the celebration of the Church the Christ event is recalled with thanksgiving and petition is made for the bestowal of its benefits on all people. As ritual-liturgical proclamation of Christ, he himself is present in it and through it granting communion with himself and uniting the Church to his intercession before the Father (E5-8). In the light of this intercessory aspect Catholic theology's application of the concept "propitiatory sacrifice" to the eucharist may be

understood as a reference to the liturgical presentation before the Father of the one expiation of the
cross in the intercession of Christ and the Church for
humanity (ECom 8).

The text alludes to the anamnēsis prayer which
follows the narrative of institution of the eucharist
in most traditional liturgies of the East and West. A
commentary on this prayer is given as a comparison with
a typical anamnēsis prayer shows. Roman Canon III of
the Missale Romanum of Paul VI can serve as an example.

E 9-10	Roman Canon III
"The anamnesis of Christ is the basis and source of all Christian prayer. ... In the eucharist, Christ empowers us to live with him, to suffer with him and to pray through him as justified sinners, joyfully and freely fulfilling his will" (E9). "In Christ we offer ourselves as a living and holy sacrifice in our daily lives... "(E10).	"Father, calling to mind the death your Son endured for our salvation,...his resurrection and ascension...and ready to greet him when he comes again, we offer you in thanksgiving this holy and living sacrifice..."

According to the text of the agreed statement the
anamnēsis prayer contains the idea that by recalling
the Christ-event and its consequences for us, we are
able to offer ourselves to the Father in Christ as a
living and holy sacrifice.

Two other allusions to the text of traditional
eucharistic prayers are included in this section. The
commemoration of the saints and martyrs is viewed as
the expression of the Church's conviction that it
worships in communion with the heavenly Church (E11).
The liturgical recitation of the account of institution
is the Church's confession of Christ's "real, living
and active presence in the eucharist," fulfilling his
promise to communicate himself in the bread and wine:
"the sacrament of his real presence." This real
presence is not dependent on the faith of the individual, according to the text. This implies that it is a
real presence in the community as such (E13). Commentary (13) contrasts the belief of "many churches" that
a transempirical change takes place in the reality of
the bread and wine with that of "some churches" which
do not associate Christ's real presence to the bread
and wine in the same way. Finally the verbal preaching

at the eucharist is recommended since it reinforces the ritual-liturgical proclamation of Christ (E12).

3) The eucharist is invocation of the Spirit (E14-18). As act of the Church the eucharist is the liturgical response to the command of Christ and also the petition for the coming of the Spirit to fulfill the promise contained in Christ's command. But what the Church does by way of remembrance and petition serves as transparency for what the Father, Incarnate Son and Holy Spirit are doing in and through the liturgical celebration.

As act of faith of the Church, of which the Spirit is the living source, the ritual-liturgical proclamation is distinguished from the contingent historical reality of the Last Supper and sacrifice of the cross. But the Christ event, because of its eschatological value, presents itself in and through the celebration. The meal of the Church shares in the truth of the Christ event in the sense that it mediates the gift of the crucified and risen Lord "in the Spirit," i.e., in the power of the Spirit.

The theological explanation of the role of the Spirit, given in the text of BEM, can be paraphrased in the following way. The Church recalls the enduring promise of the Last Supper in the Spirit; the risen Lord relates his promise to this eucharist. The Church relates its bread and wine to the promise of the Last Supper in the Spirit; the risen Lord relates the bread and wine of the Church to that of the Last Supper. What the Spirit does through the expression of the faith of the Church corresponds to what Christ does because of the union between the Son and the Spirit. Because the Spirit, who works through the Church, relates the bread and wine of the Church to Christ's self-offering they become realizing signs of it; because Christ gives himself in bread and wine to the community they are realizing signs of his self gift. But Christ gives himself in bread and wine to the community as the giver of life to the world. Therefore this sharing of bread and wine is sacrament of the communication of the Father's love in Christ. The Father, in turn, communicates the Holy Spirit in a purely transcendental act by which the Church receives "the life of the new creation," a pledge of the fulfillment of the kingdom (E14-18).

Commentary (15) lists three approaches to the idea that bread and wine "become the sacramental signs of

Christ's body and blood." The first two correspond to the different beliefs of the churches found in Commentary (13). The third mentions theological explanations, associated with either of the two beliefs of churches, which seek to protect the real presence from "damaging interpretations." Thereby it is implied that the ecumenical problem is reduced to the different beliefs of churches mentioned in Commentary (13).

Commentary (14) points out that, as activity of the Church, the eucharist is a prayer addressed to the Father for the fulfillment of the promise of the Last Supper through the sending of the Spirit. This corresponds to the understanding of the early liturgies that the whole "prayer action" brings about the reality promised by Christ and offers as possible solution to the historical debate about a "special moment of consecration."

4) The eucharist is communion of the faithful (E19-21). In the eucharist the local church actualizes itself as the body of Christ and so, in communion with Christ, the participants manifest and deepen their union with one another. Since the local church represents the whole Church in its eucharist and worships on behalf of the whole world, the responsibility of its members to promote communion with other local churches and to contribute to the spiritual and temporal welfare of all humanity comes to the foreground. This responsibility finds a variety of expressions in the liturgy itself.

Commentary (19) affirms the principle that baptism incorporates the believer into the body of Christ and so grounds the right to full participation in the eucharist of the Church. Two comments are made on this principle. The first refers directly to the relation between the local eucharist and the whole Church which is mentioned in E19. The catholicity of the eucharist, i.e., its quality as manifestation of the whole Church is "less manifest" when the right of baptized and their ministers to participate and preside over eucharistic celebration in one church is not recognized by the members and officials of another church. Also the problem of excluding baptized children from the eucharist, a practice of some churches, is raised on the grounds that baptism gives a fundamental right to the eucharist.

5) The eucharist is the meal of the kingdom (E22-26). The eucharistic thanksgiving to God for the

139

signs of renewal of the world and the anticipation of the coming of the kingdom offer a vision of the fulfillment. The eucharistic assembly represents all creation in its intercession for renewal. Through the eucharist the community is nourished to serve as agent of reconciliation in the world and witness to the coming kingdom. The celebration itself is a participation in God's mission of preaching the gospel of the kingdom, service to the neighbor and witness of fidelity. Through the eucharist Christians are equipped to confess Christ and so draw others into the eucharistic assembly. But insofar as Christians themselves cannot ignite together at the eucharist their missionary witness is weakened.

III. The Celebration of the Eucharist (E27-33). A list of typical elements found historically in the eucharistic liturgies is given. The thanksgiving prayer addressed to the Father is linked to the Jewish berakah and the traditional anamnēsis prayer is described without reference to the prayer of offering which it contains (E27). These aspects are singled out for comment in the second part of this essay.

The suggestion is made that all churches should test their liturgies in the light of the growing "eucharistic agreement." But common eucharistic faith is not judged to imply uniformity in liturgy or practices (E28). The twofold role of the presiding minister, an ordained person "in most churches," is mentioned: representation of Christ and of the connection between local eucharistic communities (29). Frequent celebration of the eucharist is recommended because it deepens Christian faith. As celebration of the resurrection, it should take place every Sunday (E30-31). Reservation of the sacrament by some churches is linked to their "stress" on Christ's continued presence in the consecrated elements. This is contrasted with the practice of other churches which place "the main emphasis" on the act of celebration and reception of the elements in the liturgy (32). Commentary (28) cites the opinion of some that local food and drink might serve better than bread and wine "to anchor the eucharist in everyday life" in places where the traditional elements are not commonly found.

Finally, the text closes with the observation that more extended eucharistic sharing between separated churches may be possible on the basis of the "increased mutual understanding" expressed in the document. This activity is viewed as a possible contribution to the realization of the unity of all churches around a common eucharist (E33).

PART II

The following commentary on selected topics of our summary of the eucharist section of the Lima text follows the division of Part I.

I.   The Institution of the Eucharist

1) The description of the origin of the eucharist provides an adequate preliminary statement of the New Testament witness to the continuity and discontinuity between the meals of Jesus' public life, the Last Supper, the resurrection meals and the eucharist of the Church. Any further elaboration must include, above all, additional differentiation among these meals: the open-ended meals of Jesus' public life at which none were excluded, the closed circle of the Last Supper, the corresponding closed circle of the resurrection meals, and the eucharist of the Church.

The discontinuity seems to be historically grounded on the rejection of Jesus' message of God's unconditional offer of reconciliation to all by Israel as representative of humanity. This created the new situation in which Jesus became conscious of his role to expiate for this sin of rejection by his obedience unto death as representative of humanity. At the Last Supper Jesus reveals to his disciples, through symbolic words and action, that through affirming the meaning of his death and its consequences in faith, one obtains a share in the new covenant. In the resurrection meals the risen Lord reveals himself. In this revelatory event the gift of faith to respond to his saving presence is communicated.

An important consequence follows from this: the eucharist of the Church is open only to those who are members of the Church and who affirm faith in the saving death of Jesus. The new offer of reconciliation made in the eucharist is universal, as was the original offer made in the preaching of Jesus' public life. Christ died for all! However, this gift comes through the preaching of the Church in and by which Christ himself preaches himself. Hence the new paschal meal is only open to those who believe in Christ and are united to his body, the Church.

2)   The   command   of   Christ: "Do   this   in
remembrance of me," is not explicitly predicated of the
historical Jesus.   This accords with the current state
of investigation of the history of tradition of the
narratives   of   institution.   However,   the   command   is
interpreted to mean: do this as a remembrance of me.
Thereby it is brought into line with a Jewish theology
of the Passover feast.   But from the standpoint of
exegesis another option is open.   The command could
mean: do this in order that God may remember me and
bring the fulfillment of the kingdom.

The   first   interpretation   stresses   the
actualization of the Christ event for the benefit of
the participants; the second places the emphasis on the
idea that the celebration of a liturgical rite, established by divine institution, awakens God's remembrance
of his promises.   The latter understanding also has a
Jewish   background.   Moreover   it   corresponds   to   the
early Christian lively expectation of the proximity of
the second coming of Christ as expressed in Didache 10:
"Let grace come, and the world pass away."

Any further elaboration of the eucharistic text
might include the latter option and, at the same time,
show how neither interpretation contradicts the theological content of the other.   Here would be the place
to introduce the theology of preaching of the New
Testament, especially as found in Paul.   The ritual-liturgical proclamation of the Christ event is no
less efficacious than the verbal preaching.   In both
forms Christ preaches himself and offers a share in his
redemptive sacrifice to the hearers.   Thereby they are
enabled to carry on the mission of Christ, in union
with Christ, until he comes: "I have sent them into the
world as you sent me" (Jn 17:18).   Consequently the
effect of the ritual-liturgical proclamation of Christ
corresponds to that of the Passover meal in which the
memorial of the original redemptive work of Yahweh is
understood to include its actualization for the benefit
of the covenant community.

On the other hand, the liturgical representation
of   the   Christ   event   by   the   Church   stresses   the
definitive nature of the sacrifice of Christ.   It is a
ritual-liturgical form of intercession of the community
before   the   Father   for   the   fulfillment   of   what   is
already realized in Christ as representative of humanity.   As a petition of the Church before God to fulfill
his promises, made in union with Jesus Christ, it is
calculated to arouse a lively hope in the second coming

of Christ for those who have accepted the implications of the incorporation into Christ. It seems inappropriate that the Lima text on eucharist, which continually mentions the eschatological aspect of the eucharist, arbitrarily limits the original understanding of anamnēsis in the command of Christ to the recall of the community and the corresponding actualization of what is remembered for the benefit of the community here and now.

II. <u>The Meaning of the Eucharist</u>. No special remarks are needed on the initial description of the essential meaning of the eucharist and the aspect of thanksgiving directed to the Father. However from the standpoint of Roman Catholic tradition several observations can be made on the remainder of this section.

1) <u>The eucharist as memorial of Christ</u> (nos. 5-13). Seven themes are singled out for comment: active presence of Christ, propitiatory sacrifice, relation between Christ's active and somatic presence, dependence of Christ's presence on the community of faith, the <u>anamnēsis</u> offering prayer, commemoration of the saints, liturgical preaching.

(1) Active Presence of Christ, the High Priest. The text stresses the active presence of Christ in the eucharist. He is present as High Priest who unites the community to his unique sacrifice and who, as a consequence, communicates self to the community in the sacrificial elements of bread and wine. This approach corresponds to the movement of the liturgy from sacrificial prayer to sacramental communion of the body and blood. It likewise conforms to patristic theology which grounds the mystery of the eucharist in the actual presence of the sacrifice of the cross and the corresponding communion with the crucified and risen Lord through the sacramental food and drink.

(2) Propitiatory Sacrifice. The explanation of the application of the use of propitiatory sacrifice to the eucharist, found in Commentary (8), corresponds to a traditional scholastic eucharistic theology. Here it is explained that in the memorial the Church offers the sacrifice of Christ in the sense that it presents it, in union with Christ, to the Father and so pleads for the application of the propitiatory effects of the one expiation of the cross, made concrete in the intercessions. The liturgical grounds for this explanation is found in the <u>anamnēsis</u> offering which states

that recalling the Christ event "we offer to you, God ... this holy and perfect sacrifice" (Roman Canon I).

This explanation can be called into question on two counts. First, it is difficult to see why it does not make the eucharist an independent sacrificial act which competes with the unique sacrifice of the cross offered once for all. It gives the impression that the sacrifice of Christ is now offered again (iterum) liturgically by Christ and the Church. Second, it is doubtful that the interpretation corresponds to the original intention of this ancient anamnēsis prayer.

According to Catholic theology the sacrifice of the cross is sacramentally present in the eucharist in order that its propitiatory effects may be applied to the participants and those for whom intercession is made. So the eucharist is propitiatory because it is an application of the one expiation of the cross. Intercession is a concrete way of application of the expiation of the cross in the eucharistic liturgy. However, a part of the common Catholic eucharistic theology also teaches that the eucharist is a propitiatory sacrifice because it effects propitiation as "a true and proper sacrifice." This was reaffirmed at the Council of Trent. In other words, each eucharist is a propitiatory sacrifice not simply because it is a rite of application of the one expiation of the cross. Rather because each eucharist is a rite of offering, it is a rite of application of the fruits of the cross. Offering is the way of application of the benefits of the cross. But how is this to be explained in such a way that the integrity of the unique High Priestly act of Christ on the cross is maintained?

Within Roman Catholic theology the problem can be approached by beginning with the role of the ordained minister in the eucharistic liturgy. [1] Commissioned by Christ to preside at the eucharist of his Church, the ordained person acts not only in the name of the Church by observing the official ritual form of celebration but also in the name of Christ. He represents Christ's priesthood because Christ makes his sacrifice present in the act of offering by the priest and, as a consequence, applies the one expiation of the cross to the faithful. But this act of offering of the priest in no way competes with the once-for-all sacrificial offering of the one High Priest. In essence the act of offering of the priest is the official ritual-liturgical proclamation of the memorial of the Lord.

144

In other words it is the offering of the sacrifice of Christ to the community as a grace of God by preaching. It is a priestly ministry in the Pauline sense (Rom 15:16) by which the sacrifice of Christ is applied to the community. Through this offering Christ himself draws the community into his sacrifice so that it is made an acceptable offering to God.

There is also a ritual acceptance of this offering of the sacrifice of Christ to the community through the official priestly act of ritual-liturgical proclamation. Moreover this ritual acceptance is an offering. In the anamnēsis offering prayer the priest offers Christ's sacrifice to the Father in his own name and that of the community. This act of offering is not one of returning the gift to the Father as though the Church had no need of it. Moreover, it is not a new presentation of the sacrifice of Christ, by Christ and the Church, which adds something to the efficacy of the one sacrifice of the cross. Rather it is a way of application of the sacrifice of the cross to the community. In other words it is the grateful acknowledgement that the gift of God remains a gift though given to us.

The Church must continually recall and confess that the gift of God in Christ is one which we neither merit by human works nor possess as our own inalienable property once it is given. In the eucharist, in the liturgical "use" of this gift on which our lives depend, the proper way of acceptance is to offer it to God as the liturgical expression of total dependence of the community on the gift. This understanding of the anamnēsis offering of the sacrifice of Christ seems to conform to the patristic and early liturgical sources. The evidence for this is given under (5) of this section, "anamnēsis offering prayer and Christian self-offering."

In this perspective the intercessory prayer for the living and dead, characteristic of the eucharist, is explainable on the basis that in the eucharist the sacrifice of Christ is offered by the priestly ministry to the community so that it is drawn into Christ's worship. In intimate union with the acceptable worship of Christ, the Church brings its petitions before the Father in the certainty that the High Priest intercedes for it.

(3) Christ's Active and Somatic Presence. The text correctly stresses the active presence of Christ

145

who gives himself in bread and wine. But how is one to approach the problem of the relation between Christ's active presence and his self-communication in and through the elements of bread and wine? How is the intrinsic relation between the two forms of Christ's presence to be explained? Only a relational ontology seems adequate today to provide an approach to Christ's somatic presence which secures, at the same time, the conviction that Christ actually gives himself to us by his own hand and that we actually receive him from his hands in our own hands. [2]

Within modern Catholic eucharistic theology, insofar as grounded on a rational ontology, the relation between Christ's active and somatic real presence is approached in the following way. In the eucharist Christ makes the bread and wine realizing signs of his self-communication. Thereby they obtain a new meaning. Christ places them in the relation between himself and his community. The change of being, an ontological change, takes place within the earthly bread and wine. They become sacramental signs of Christ's self-offering and yet remain subject to the earthly laws of corporeality. So there are two dimensions to one and the same undivided reality.

These two dimensions do not correspond to the two principles of being of the scholastic doctrine of transubstantiation: substance and accidents. Rather they correspond to the distinction between being and its relationality. All being is essentially relational. The being itself is formally distinct from the realizations of its relatedness to other beings but at the same time really identified with these relations. The relatedness is realized when a reality is given meaning through human or divine intentionality. So a reality is not constituted through substantial and accidental reality but through the relational connections in which the reality as such stands.

Within this perspective one can speak of a real change of the reality of bread and wine in the eucharist even if they remain what they were as physical realities. The one dimension remains (physical magnitude), while the other changes (anthropological magnitude). The basic distinction between the eucharist and other sacraments which employ material elements lies in the fact that water or oil do not become the sacramant. Rather the symbolic actions accomplished with them are the sacraments.

Whether this approach to the problem of Christ's active and somatic real presence will receive further support within Catholic theology and in the dialogue between the churches remains an open question. However, an opening to this approach in the dialogue between churches may be found in a comparison between the relation of the witness of Scripture to the event of revelation and the relation of the sharing of bread and wine to Christ's self-communication.

The witness of Scripture is related to what is witnessed by it (the event of revelation) and is related to the one who witnesses to himself in it (the risen Lord). The witness of Scripture is not the event of revelation. Rather it is relational to the event. At the same time it is absolute in the sense that Christ himself interprets himself in the witness of Scripture. The sharing of the eucharistic elements is related to what is signified by it (Christ's self-communication) and is related to the one who signifies through it (Christ, the host of the meal). The sharing of bread and wine is relational to Christ's self-communication to the community. At the same time it is absolute in the sense that Christ himself relates himself to this point of reference without at the same time being dependent on it. For it is not the community which submits Christ to this point of reference but Christ himself, as the accounts of institution indicate.

(4) Dependence of Christ's Presence on the Community of Faith. The text states that Christ's presence does not depend on the faith of the individual. Thereby it is implied that it depends on the assembly of believers. This latter theme is not developed. According to Roman Catholic theology Christ's eucharistic presence is conditioned by the intention of the community of faith, which can call itself church, to assemble for the meal under the commission of Christ.

The community must intend to receive what Christ intends to give through the meal of his Church. Both the eucharistic faith of the community which corresponds to the meaning of the eucharist from its origin and the commissioning of the community by Christ as local realization of his Church are constitutive of the eucharist. Here the problem of the structure of the community which can mediate the commission of Christ in the Church through history is raised. If Christ commissions official representatives, through

ordination, by those who have received the same
sacramental commissioning to act as ministerial host at
his table, only communities which have such officials
are assured that the relation between Christ as host
and the community as guests is realized.

(5) Anamnēsis Offering Prayer and Christian
Self-Offering. The text alludes to the anamnēsis
offering prayer and links it to the self-offering of
Christians: the spiritual worship of daily life, which
is nourished by the eucharist. In the comments on
propitiatory sacrifice it was indicated that the
anamnēsis offering prayer originally had the meaning of
thankful acknowledgement of the gift of the sacrifice
of Christ. However, this act includes, by its very
nature, the self-offering of Christians.

The anamnēsis offering prayer, after the account
of institution, is found in traditional Eastern and
Western liturgies, the exception in the East is the
Alexandrian type which refers the oblation to the
earlier ritual presentation of the gifts. Luther,
Zwingli and Calvin objected to the idea expressed in
this prayer because the gift (sacramentum) requires
acceptance and not return (sacrificium). In an
ecumenical age the Roman Catholic Church has not
dropped the anamnēsis offering prayer in the new
eucharistic prayers of the Missale Romanum of Paul VI.
Moreover in related documents great stress is placed on
the idea that the Church offers Christ in the celebration of the eucharist.

According to modern official Roman Catholic
theology the offering of Christ's sacrifice by the
Church takes place at the moment of the sacramental
representation of the sacrifice of the cross, i.e., at
the recitation of the account of institution when the
priest acts in persona Christi. At this moment the
bread and wine are transformed into the body and blood
of Christ. Hence the transubstantiation of the bread
and wine coincides temporally with the sacramental
representation of the sacrifice of the cross. At this
moment the Church appropriately unites itself to the
once-for-all sacrificial act of Christ sacramentally
present. The anamnēsis offering, which follows the
recitation of the account of institution, is generally
interpreted as a kind of affirmation of what takes
place at the moment of consecration when the Church
unites itself in faith with the offering of Christ
himself made visible in the act of the priest and so
offers itself in, with and through Christ.

Recent official Roman Catholic documents clearly distinguish between two activities of the faithful: they offer Christ and they offer themselves. Vatican II's Constitution on the Liturgy states that the "Church desires that the faithful ... give thanks to God, offer the immaculate victim, not only by the hands of the priest, but also together with him, learn to offer themselves" (48). The offering "by the hands of the priest" refers to the moment of consecration when the faithful spiritually unite themselves to the offering of Christ and so offer themselves in union with Christ. The idea that the faithful learn to offer themselves in union with the priest seems to allude to the anamnēsis offering prayer wherein the priest expresses in his own name and that of the Church the intention of self-offering. Vatican II's Decree on the Ministry of Presbyters instructs presbyters to "teach the faithful to offer the divine victim to God the Father in the sacrifice of the Mass and to make the offering of their lives with it" (5). Here the close connection between the offering of Christ and self-offering is made. The one implies the other. Also the General Instruction on the Roman Missal of Paul VI explains that the "Church ... offers the spotless victim to the Father in the Holy Spirit ... the faithful not only offer this victim but also learn to offer themselves" (55-56).

The meaning of "offering Christ" is explained by the Catholic partners in no. 58 of the Roman Catholic/Lutheran Agreed Statement on the Eucharist in accord with the teaching of official Catholic theology: "Of ourselves we cannot offer to God praise ... but we offer Christ: He is praise ... . It is this act of testifying to one's own powerlessness ... which is intended when the Catholic Church dares to say that not only Christ offers himself for humanity, but that the Church also 'offers' him." [3] Here "offering Christ" is interpreted to mean that the Church presents liturgically the sacrifice of Christ before the Father as the uniquely acceptable worship.

This interpretation is certainly conformed to the theology of the eucharist insofar as it stresses the unique value of the sacrifice of the cross and so the correspondingly absolute need of uniting ourselves to the worship of Christ in order that our worship may be accepted by the Father. Hence the concept of "offering Christ" is brought into conformity with the dogma of justification by faith alone - a concern of the Lutheran partners of the dialogue. However, the whole

149

liturgical tradition of the anamnēsis offering prayer does not focus on the powerlessness of the Church to offer acceptable worship apart from Christ. Rather it stresses the offering of the gift of Christ to the Father who is source of the gift.

The traditional theology behind the anamnēsis offering prayer can be traced back to the second century. Irenaeus understands that God instituted sacrifice for human need. It is a returning to God of God's gift to show gratitude. Of course, Irenaeus does not think that God repossesses the gift. In the context of the rejection by Gnostics of the value of the material world, Irenaeus says that Christians offer to God what he has created and owns: "We offer to him his own." [4] This concept is found in a passage of Irenaeus which refers to the oblation of the Church in the eucharist: the oblation includes, along with the whole of creation, the eucharistic gifts. [5]

Irenaeus draws on a biblical concept, directly or indirectly, which is frequently paraphrased in ancient Church inscriptions. This also holds true for the old Roman Canon's reference to the offering "de tuis donis ac datis." While the phrase refers to all God's gifts it especially is concerned with the gift of the altar. The Byzantine anaphoras of Chrysostom and Basil have a similar expression which is as old as that of the Roman Canon: "Offering to you what is yours out of what is yours, in all and for all." The gift offered is above all the eucharistic bread and wine as an early witness to the Latin anamnēsis prayer makes clear: "We offer to you this spotless victim, spiritual victim, unbloody victim, this holy bread and cup of eternal life." [6]

In the deepest theological sense to offer Christ to the Father means to confess that the gift belongs to God precisely because it is a gift. It is the confession that the gift is not our possession but always remains gift. It expresses the total dependence of the recipients on God. At the same time it is a thankful acceptance of the gift. It expresses the spiritual openness of the recipients to receive God's self-communication in Christ. But this acceptance in thanksgiving is sacrifice. The self-offering of Christians to God consists essentially in their openness to receive the meaning of their lives by freely accepting the sacrifice of Christ as its basis and source. This self-offering, with all its consequences, is necessarily included in the acceptance of Christ with thanksgiving. Therefore it includes the openness to be messengers of reconciliation in the world: to be in the world "for the world." It is by this total acceptance of the gift of Christ that Christians remain open: their spiritual sacrifice, to receive the meaning of their lives from the Father. However, a thankful acceptance, by its nature, must also include the offering of what is accepted to God: Christ. It expresses the spiritual attitude, the sacrificial attitude, which recognizes God's gift as gift.

The text of BEM interprets the anamnēsis offering prayer as the expression of the self-offering of Christians in union with Christ. This is correct insofar as it points to what is ultimately signified by the rite of offering the gift of Christ to the Father with thanksgiving. What is ultimately signified by the amen to the offering of Jesus' sacrifice to the Father as gift is the thankful acceptance of this gift: the self-offering of Christians which consists in the openness to freely receive the gift which gives meaning to one's life. But at the level of the liturgical prayer this self-offering is precisely signified by the grateful acceptance expressed by offering the sacrifice of Jesus as gift of the Father to the Father.

(6) Commemoration of the Saints. The text interprets the traditional liturgical commemoration of the saints and martyrs as expression of the Church's conviction of its communion with the heavenly Church in its worship. No reference is made to the petition for the intercession of the saints on behalf of the earthly Church which is included either explicitly or implicitly in the commemoration. According to Augustine, and the Western tradition, the saints and martyrs are mentioned because we need their intercession. However, since eucharist refers to intercessory prayer of the earthly Church which, through Christ, finds favor before God, this affords an opening to the idea of intercession of saints for the pilgrim Church.

(7) Verbal Preaching. According to the text verbal preaching of the anamnēsis of Christ at the eucharist is fitting since it complements the ritual-liturgical proclamation. A stronger reason can be given. The preaching of the word before the eucharist is needed normally because the distance between the risen Lord and the Church is bridged by the gift of faith freely given by God and accepted in freedom. The Church is receiver of the gift of Christ in the eucharist. It must receive this gift in freedom and understanding of faith. The preaching of the word

prepares the Church for full, active participation in the concise ritual-liturgical proclamation of the anamnēsis of Christ.

2) The eucharist as invocation of the Spirit (nos. 14-18). One comment may suffice for this section of the text. It concerns the approach to the problem of the special moment of consecration from the liturgical point of view. From this perspective the presiding minister speaks the whole eucharistic prayer in the name of the Church and so of Christ who is head of the Church. The theological explanation of a special moment of consecration in scholastic theology is not so orientated. It makes a sharp distinction between the eucharistic prayer and the narrative of institution. The one is recited in the name of the Church, the other in the name of Christ. This theology assumes that when the priest recites the words of Christ he does so in the name of Christ and not in the name of the Church except insofar as Christ is the head of the Church. Consequently the priest is described as acting in persona Christi and directly signifying, or denoting, Christ's act of consecrating bread and wine. Since what Christ does corresponds to what the Spirit does, there is no need of invoking the Spirit for the sanctification of the eucharistic elements.

This theological explanation overlooks the levels of signification of the liturgical rite. As the BEM text correctly observes, at the level of the visible rite the whole eucharistic prayer is one of thanksgiving and petition for the realization of the eucharistic event which is grounded on the promise of Christ expressed in the narrative of institution. But for the eyes of faith this prayer of the Church signifies, or connotes, the action of Christ and the Spirit. For it is made in faith of which Christ in the Spirit is the living source.

The eucharistic prayer both manifests the unity between the Church and Christ and the distinction between the Church and Christ. Only in thanksgiving to the Father for the gift of Christ does the Church speak the eucharistic words of Christ and so receive the gift of the Father's love. The Church does not dare to give the impression that it acts immediately in place of Christ. Through the thanksgiving prayer it makes its relation of dependence on the true host of the meal visible in the rite.

Because of the distance between Christ and the Church effected by his glorification, a direct copying of the New Testament version of the Last Supper is out of the question. It would not sufficiently situate the Church as thankful recipient in the diaspora situation of the pilgrim people of God in which Christ is present in the Spirit and absent in the flesh. This practice could also lead to eating and drinking without discerning the consequence of accepting the way of the cross implied in the sharing of the sacrifice of Christ in the eucharist. But the placing of the priest on the side of Christ over against the community in the recitation of the narrative of institution tends to dissolve the distance between Christ and the community. The equating of the eucharist with the Last Supper by interpreting the priest's action at the recitation of the narrative of institution as denoting the action of Christ historizes the eucharistic liturgy. It makes of it an act of Christ in the Church which corresponds to the act of Jesus at the Last Supper. The difference consists in the fact that the risen Lord acts through his commissioned minister.

This theological understanding could and did lead to the omission of the eucharist prayer in some Reformation liturgies. But this practice contradicts the liturgical witness that the eucharist is an act of the Church of which Christ in the Spirit is source. As act of the Church the eucharist is the thankful response of faith to the gift of Christ. The thankful response corresponds to the gift and, furthermore, is the liturgical way in which and through which the gift is bestowed on the community.

3) The Eucharist as Communion of the Faithful (nos. 19-21). In this section Commentary (19) calls for some discussion. It refers to the catholicity of the eucharist which is less manifest when one church refuses to recognize the right of another church to celebrate the eucharist. This way of stating the problem seems to be too imprecise.

The refusal of one church to recognize the right of another Christian community to celebrate the eucharist bears on the essential relation between church and eucharist. As a refusal to recognize the other Christian community as truly church, qualified to celebrate the eucharist, the catholicity of that community, i.e., its quality as manifestation of the whole Church, and consequently the catholicity of its eucharist is "less manifest." But to whom?

153

In the eyes of the church which refuses recognition, the catholicity of the community in question, and its eucharist is not manifest. The "less manifest" must refer to the community which is refused the status of church. If it recognizes the right of a church to celebrate the eucharist which refuses it the same right, then the catholicity of its eucharist, with reference to the church which refuses recognition, becomes "less manifest" to it.

Commentary (19) also refers to the problem of exclusion of baptized children as communicants at the table of the Lord. Since the patristic period some Western churches have delayed eucharistic communion until children have acquired some understanding of the meaning of the whole celebration.

On this subject it suffices to note that the fundamental right of baptized infants to the eucharist can be balanced off against the pastoral concern for the personal appropriation of the whole content of the eucharist. In the eucharist the Christ event is present in its inner continuity: the utter fidelity of Christ unto death which expressed its fulfillment in the resurrection. It is made accessible to the community so that it is taken up in faith into the relationship of obedience and love of Christ before the Father. Christians who begin to live the life of faith by personal appropriation of it need the eucharist by which they are continually drawn into Christ's obedience before the Father. Since the eucharist is "one complete act" which includes both the self-offering of Christians in, with and through the sacrifice of Christ and communion of the sacrificed body and blood of Christ, it is reasonable to delay participation in communion until the baptized person can "somehow" actually participate in the whole liturgical act.

4) The Eucharist as Meal of the Kingdom (nos. 22-26). Although sufficiently indicated elsewhere in the Lima text on the eucharist, at this point the text might have stressed that the eucharist, as meal of the kingdom, has its meaning in itself. It is not simply a means of nourishment for the daily life of faith. It is the meal of the risen Lord with his Church, the anticipation of the banquet of the kingdom. Christ is present in the eucharist to ground a community in which the kingdom is made visible.

Insofar as assembly of the Church, the eucharist is also mission, as the text points out. Christ

154

assembles his community at one point in order to send it to all people. He gives himself in the eucharist to be given in turn by believers to the world. So the preaching of Christ to all people has a eucharistic background. Christ also assembles the community in order to send it back into the world to live in fidelity to the way of the cross for its own salvation. Only by trial in the world is the goal reached by the individual for which the eucharist gives hope and strength.

III. The Celebration of the Eucharist (E27-33).

1) The text lists a series of elements found in eucharistic liturgies of various traditions. Perhaps too much stress is placed on the connection between the Jewish berakah and the eucharistic prayer (E27; cf. also E3). The structure of ancient eucharistic prayers is not certainly immediately derived from the Jewish berakah. Rather it seems to be related to a much broader traditional structure of Jewish prayer which is based on covenant theology. The two basic forms of this type of prayer account for two types of eucharistic prayer in which the narrative of institution is situated in the anamnestic or epicletic sections. [7]

The Lima text's reference to the anamnēsis prayer omits any reference to the offering of the sacrifice of Christ which it traditionally includes. Since this prayer still provides difficulties for some Reformation churches, some explanation of how it could be understood so as to meet the objections of the Reformers would have been useful. One approach to the problem is given in Part II, 2 (2), (5) of this essay.

2) The role of the presiding minister as representative of Christ is mentioned. But can more be said than that the minister "represents the divine initiative?" The BEM text of ministry provides material which can furnish an adequate response to this question.

According to Lima document (M17) the ordained minister can be called priest because he fulfills a priestly service ... "through word and sacrament." Commentary (17) of that same document refers to Rom 15:16 where Paul speaks of his priestly service of the gospel. From this standpoint it can be said that the ordained minister's official ritual-liturgical proclamation of the anamnēsis of Christ is a priestly service: a way of application of Christ's sacrifice to the community. Also the offering of Christ to the Father with thanksgiving in the _anamnēsis_ offering prayer is a priestly service of the gospel. It is a way of expressing that the ordained minister's priestly service and that of the common priesthood of all believers is totally dependent on Christ. Insofar as the community makes this prayer its own, it is the way of application of the sacrifice of Christ to the community.

3) The text bases the frequency of the eucharist on the fact that it deepens the life of faith. This should be complemented by noting the function of the eucharist to manifest and realize church. The importance of the ecclesiological dimension of the eucharist is also a basic reason for frequency of celebration.

4) The reservation of the eucharist by some churches is said to be grounded on the conviction of Christ's continued presence in the consecrated elements after the consecration. But what is the theological basis of this conviction? The document emphasizes the eschatological dimension of the eucharist which actually grounds the reason for reservation.

The eucharist is anticipation of the heavenly banquet and the food and drink are the anticipated self-gift of Christ of the kingdom. Moreover the Church exists outside the celebration as sign of the coming gathering into the kingdom. Christ gives himself fully in the bread and wine of the eucharist; the consecrated elements become the crystallized form of the self-offering of his life for us and to us.

Why should we think that Christ withdraws his presence after the temporal moment of the liturgical celebration from the elements which remain? When Christ relates himself to this concrete point of reference in the celebration in a definitive way, does the Church have any other option than to believe the elements remain sacrament of his self-giving after the celebration? Only a purely functional interpretation of the sharing of bread and wine with respect to Christ's real presence cannot cope with the idea of reservation. Here the act of sharing does not concern the bread and wine themselves but only their function for us, i.e., to assure us that the risen Lord is present as savior.

5) Commentary (28) refers to the possibility of using other elements than bread and wine in parts of the world where they are not customary or obtainable. Those who favor this argue that it anchors the eucharist in everyday life in a better way.

All sacraments which employ material elements draw them from daily life where thay have a symbolic meaning appropriate to what is being signified. Only in this way does the symbolic action involving material elements convey meaning. Moreover, in the history of religions various forms of food and drink have been taken up and used in ritual meals to express enduring values which underlie the daily lives of religious communities.

Consequently from the anthropological point of view it is conceivable that in certain cultures the use of traditional food and drink might better serve to express the meaning of the eucharist. The main objections against this position can be grouped under two headings: the christological dimension of the eucharist; the symbolic function of bread and wine.

(1) Christological dimension. First there is the command of Christ: "Do this ... ." It is difficult to imagine that churches which believe this command came from Jesus at the Last Supper, or though the risen Lord working in his Church, will assume responsibilty for changing the food and drink of the Last Supper. Second, Christ is the host of the meal. He invites believers to his table to share in his food. Will this not be obscured if we decide what food and drink are to be used?

(2) Symbolic Function of Bread and Wine. First, the symbolic action of the eucharist is related to the contingent historical event of the Last Supper. By the use of bread and wine this real relation of the eucharist to the Last Supper is indicated. In other words the bread and wine have an index function. An index has a real relation to something which is absent (e.g., a footprint in the sand). If other food and drink are used this index function is not as evident and thereby the link between eucharist and Last Supper is obscured. Second, Christ employed bread and wine as symbols of his body and blood given for the salvation of the world. In so doing he used elements which had a symbolic meaning in first century Jewish culture appropriate to what is being signified. This raises a practical problem: what food and drink in a particular

culture are appropriate to convey the meaning given by Christ to bread and wine?

6) The text closes (E33) with a reference to possible eucharistic sharing between separated churches as a means of fostering the unity of the whole Church. This possibility is not envisioned by a church which holds to an exclusive ecclesiology. It assumes that there is one communion of churches which is simply identified with the body of Christ. Hence the eucharistic celebrations of this communion are the manifestation of the perfect unity of the whole Church. Since no church exists outside this communion the idea of using the eucharist to foster the unity of churches makes no sense.

The possibility of using the eucharist to foster the unity between separated churches is conceivable only where one assumes that one's own communion of churches is not simply identified with the body of Christ. In this case the eucharistic celebrations of one's communion of churches must be interpreted as a defective manifestation of the unity of the whole Church. In this context of understanding it is incorrect to say that because the eucharist is the manifestation of the perfect unity of the Church, it cannot be used as a means of fostering the unity of the separated Christian communities. Rather one must say that to the extent that separated churches are able to overcome the essential differences which preclude eucharistic sharing as a means of fostering the unity of the whole Church, their shared eucharists are a more perfect manifestations and realization of the fundamental unity of the local eucharistic communities of the universal Church.

Since Vatican II the Roman Catholic Church no longer thinks of itself as simply identified with the body of Christ. It formally recognizes other churches as churches in the full sense of eucharistic communities, notably the Eastern Orthodox and Ancient Oriental Churches. Therefore it cannot appeal to the principle of exclusive ecclesiology which argues that because the eucharist is the sign of the perfect unity of the Church, the use of the eucharist to foster unity between separated churches is excluded. The consequences of a new inclusive ecclesiology have yet to be worked out in the matter of eucharistic sharing between the Roman Catholic Church and other churches which are not in full communion with it. But the possibility of such sharing cannot be excluded automatically.

Theologians and others in positions of authority in the Roman Catholic Church should carefully verify both whether they correctly understand the official beliefs of other Christian churches about the eucharist and whether they comprehend what is determinative in those churches for designating who is to preside at the celebration of the Lord's Supper. The world confessional bodies and the Faith and Order Commission would do well to clarify what are or would be the conditions for practicing reciprocal eucharistic hospitality. Inevitably, this will require openness to the possibility of recognizing ordinations conferred in other Christian churches.

Notes for Chapter IX

1. The following analysis is dependent on Lothar Lies, "Ökumenische Erwägungen zu Abendmahl, Priesterweihe und Messopfer," Zeitschrift für katholische Theologie 104 (1982) 385-410.

2. Alexander Gerken offers a good introduction to the application of relational ontology to the presence of Christ in bread and wine of the eucharist (Theologie der Eucharistie [Munich: Kosel, 1973] 199-210). Also Gerhard Gade shows how the approach of relational ontology corresponds to the content of the agreement reached by the International Roman Catholic/Lutheran Commission in its Agreed Statement on the Eucharist, nos. 48-51 (Origins 8 (1979) 473-74): "'Das Herrenmahl' und die eucharistische Realpräsenz: Theologische Untersuchung zum ökumenischen Konsens im katholisch/lutherischen Dokument 'Das Herrenmahl'," Catholica 45 (1981) 287-317.

3. Origins 8, 474.

4. Adversus haereses IV.18,5 (Harvey IV.31,4).

5. Adversus haereses IV.18,4 (Harvey IV.29).

6. De Sacramentis VI.6,27 (CSEL 73 (1955) 57).

7. Cesare Giraudo argues rather convincingly that the Jewish berakah represents a phase, a particular form of standardization of a more ample euchological evolution in which the origin of two types of eucharistic prayer should be situated (La struttura letteraria della preghiera eucaristica: Saggio sulla genesi letteraria di'una forma toda veterotestamentaria berākā guidaica, anafora cristiana (Analecta Biblica 92; Rome: Pontifical Biblical Institute, 1981).

CHAPTER X:

THE LIMA DOCUMENT
ON ORDAINED MINISTRY

William Marrevee, S.C.J.

THE LIMA DOCUMENT
ON ORDAINED MINISTRY

William Marrevee, S.C.J.

It would be misleading to suggest that the 1982 Lima statement on the ordained ministry [1] could be considered the greatest achievement of the Commission on Faith and Order of the World Council of Churches. Such an assessment would be both exaggerated and restrictive for the simple reason that, although in the fifty-nine years of its existence the Commission has addressed a great number of issues that are part of twentieth century Church life, and although the question of the ordained ministry is perhaps the most "churchy" of these issues, it is not necessarily the most significant one. It may well be one of the more delicate issues on the ecumenical agenda, not for its own weightiness, but for what in the course of the history of division in the Church has come to be associated with it. That is also the reason why the result of Faith and Order's work as reflected in the Lima statement must not be taken lightly. That applies just as much to the member churches of the World Council of Churches as to the Roman Catholic Church, which, while not a member of the World Council of Churches, is nevertheless represented in the Commission on Faith and Order by a number of carefully selected and officially mandated theologians. Its theologians do not simply have an observer status, but are active members of the Commission and in that capacity have had a hand in shaping the document. In other words, the Roman Catholic Church is just as much an addressee of the document as are the member churches of the World Council of Churches.

The Lima document is receiving much attention, and rightly so. Not only do we see evaluations of it in theological journals, but also many creative initiatives are being undertaken to familiarize local congregations with its contents and to acclimatize them to its potential ecumenical repercussions on the life of the churches. It is particularly at this latter level that we cannot discount the significant impact the document can have and hopefully will have on the liturgical life and the polity of the churches, if the churches are prepared to move beyond an ecumenical commitment in principle.

But with all the attention being given to the Lima statement - and in this case I limit myself to the

163

section that deals with the question of the ordained ministry - , it is important to keep in mind that the Lima document does not stand alone. Many dialogues, on the regional, national and international level, have concerned themselves with the question of the ordained ministry, either in a multilateral or in a bilateral context. [2] And if at first the emergence of the bilateral dialogues might have been looked upon with a sense of apprehension by the multilateral participants because of the potential element of competition and rivalry, there is increasing evidence that the multilateral and bilateral approaches, however different, are indeed complementary and mutually enriching. [3] It should, therefore, cause no surprise if occasionally reference is made to the reports of other dialogues, either to point out the broad base of support that Faith and Order has for its stand on some aspects or to suggest the possible strengthening of its position on other aspects.

Placing the ordained ministry section of the Lima document within the broader network of the bilateral dialogue must not lead us to overlook or ignore the unique background that has led to the "final" version of the Faith and Order text. The Lima version is not an entirely new text. It incorporates positions and formulations that had been arrived at after much debate and study at the various stages that mark the long journey from Lausanne (1927) to Lima (1982). The composers of the Lima version felt themselves, in a certain sense, bound by these. In other words, the genesis and the progressive development of the text have left their marks on the final version. Apart from the fact that this makes a diachronic reading of the text along the lines of the one recently undertaken by Georg Vischer [4] possible, a synchronic reading of the text must be willing to respect the text as it is and take into account the importance of certain decisions reached in the course of the text's historical development. This also applies to the choice of the aspects under which the ministry section of the Lima document is investigated here. The choice of these aspects is dictated by what surfaced as the most contentious elements in the issue of the ordained ministry in the fifty-nine year period.

THE ORDAINED MINISTRY AND ORDINATION

In case one wonders why it is necessary to deal ecumenically with the question of the ordained ministry, the fact is that not all churches recognize the official or special ministry of the other churches. For example, the Roman Catholic Church has in fact declared Anglican Orders "invalid and entirely void." [5] Whether that judgment is correct or what the precise meaning is of such nonrecognition of the validity of Anglican Orders is another matter. As for the special ministry that in fact is operative in the Reformation churches, the closest one can come to an official Roman Catholic nonrecognition of their ministers is found in Vatican Council II's Unitatis redintegratio when it is said: "We believe they have not preserved the proper reality of the eucharistic mystery in its fulness, especially propter sacramenti Ordinis defectum." [6] This means that they have either no ministry or a deficient ministry. This nonrecognition does not apply to the Orthodox Churches, because they "yet possess true sacraments, above all – by apostolic succession – the priesthood and the Eucharist." [7] This would imply that, because of their lack of apostolic succession, the churches of the Reformation do not have a ministry or have a deficient ministry.

This negative assessment of the special ministry of the Reformation churches is part of a long estrangement between the two types of churches that for centuries has fed and been fed by a twofold popular assumption: (1) that the Reformation ministers are "only" ministers of the Word, while unique to the Roman Catholic ministers is their sacramental ministry, especially their sacrificial priesthood; and (2) that ministers in the Reformation tradition are "not more than" lay people and that they are merely delegated by their respective communities supposedly without sacramental ordination.

It is no wonder, then, that in the 1974 Accra version the Commission on Faith and Order entitled its ministry statement as "a mutually recognized ministry" [8] and the concluding chapter on the ordained ministry in the Lima document is entitled "towards the mutual recognition of the ordained ministry." [9] How then does the Lima statement propose to help the churches to clarify their position on each other's ministry? The question of method becomes important here. There are two points to make on that and they are quite decisive: (1) rather than approaching the ordained ministry in isolation, the Lima document goes to some length to spell out the christological basis and the ecclesiological context for the ordained ministry; (2) the locally experienced ecclesial fellowship in congregations or parishes - in other words, not the diocese - serves as a starting point for the articulation of the place and role of the special ministry that functions in such an ecclesial fellowship.

This methodology is not unique to the Lima document, but is employed by virtually all ecumenical documents on the question of the ordained ministry. It is a method that has proved to be very successful judging by its results, because, if the word "consensus" applies anywhere, it is to the role and place of the ordained ministry and to the meaning of ordination. This can be easily documented from all the dialogues, bilateral and multilateral, international and national. In that light, it is no exaggeration to suggest that what is ecumenically being held concerning the ordained ministry may have more than exclusively ecumenical significance and may in fact be able to contribute significantly to clearing up some strange misconceptions that mark the perception many have of the ordained ministry; it could also contribute to resolving the persisting clergy-laity split in the community of the baptized-confirmed.

When broaching the subject of the ordained ministry, the Lima document is quite emphatic in establishing the trinitarian foundation or the christological-pneumatological basis, not immediately for the ordained ministry, but for the Church. This is not just a matter of providing some interesting introductory paragraphs, but rather of making sure that the ordained ministry is not taken out of its properly ecclesiological context. One cannot move immediately from Jesus Christ to the ordained ministry; one is bound to take into account the calling of the whole people of God that actualizes, in the power of the Spirit, Christ's mission of service to the world. It is the ministry of the whole Church and of all the baptized that comes before the specific ministry of the ordained. The Lima text deals with this aspect in the first five paragraphs and then adds that if the churches are to resolve their differences concerning the place and forms of the ordained ministry they "need to work from the perspective of the calling of the whole people of God." [10]

The ordained ministry must be recognized as one of the many gifts by which the Spirit enriches the Church so that it can be built up as the body of Christ and readied for its ministry. [11] In other words, the ordained ministry cannot claim for itself the unique gift of building up the Church and serving the world to which the Church is sent. However, the fact that the ordained ministry is one of the many ministries called forth by the Spirit in the Church does not mean that it is not at the same time a special ministry given to the Church for a specific purpose. That specific purpose lies in "pointing to [the Church's] fundamental dependence on Jesus Christ and thereby providing, within a multiplicity of gifts, a focus for its unity." [12] The very presence of the ordained ministry within the community "reminds the community of the divine initiative, and of the dependence of the Church on Jesus Christ, who is the source of its mission and the foundation of its unity." [13] To describe the significance of the ordained ministry in these terms leaves no doubt that, in the eyes of the Lima document, we are dealing here with more than an organizational convenience. The very fact of the Church as a salvific reality is so much at issue in this description that the ordained ministry is said to be "constitutive for the life and witness of the Church" [14] and it is stated that "the community needs ordained ministers." [15] And if the celebration of the eucharist is indeed the most eminent actualization of the reality of the Church and if it is really Christ who presides at it, then it is incumbent upon the ordained minister to signify and represent this presidency of Christ in the celebration of the eucharist. [16] One wonders how more emphatic the point of an ordained ministry as forming part of the very structure of the Church can be made.

However unique the place and function of the ordained ministry is, the Lima document is equally emphatic in pointing out that such ordained ministry can never be thought of as being an entity unto itself. It exists only in and for the community and has no existence apart from the community. [17] Needless to say, an affirmation of this kind underlines again the ecclesial character of the ordained ministry. Once it is firmly anchored in the community, it is also imperative to ascribe to it an authority that is rooted in Jesus Christ [18] whose authority the ordained ministers manifest and exercise by a life of service modeled after that of Christ. [19] They also manifest this authority by the responsiblity they assume "to assemble and build up the Body of Christ by proclaiming and teaching the Word of God, by celebrating the sacraments, and by guiding the life of the community in its worship, its mission and its caring ministry." [20] The authority that the ordained exercise in these tasks "is not to be understood as the possession of the ordained persons, but as a gift for the continuing edification of the body in and for which the minister has been ordained." [21]

In that light, the place and task of the ordained ministers can in its basic intent, but not in its actual form, be traced to the specific authority and responsibility that Christ entrusted to the apostles. If today we can speak of leaders in the communities, then this is not to be thought of so much in a linear historical sequence going back to the apostles, but rather as Christ today choosing and calling persons through the Holy Spirit to be the leaders of the community who in that capacity "are representatives of Jesus Christ to the community." [22]

Against this background, it is appropriate to introduce the document's understanding of ordination because it is basically in line with and underlines its understanding of the place and role of the ordained ministry in the community. What must be kept in mind though is that, as may be expected, the Lima statement refrains from approaching this in ontological-juridicial categories. Its starting point here, too, is that the Church is to be understood as a christological-pneumatological reality. Within that setting it is almost self-evident to understand the liturgical act of ordination in the midst of the community, especially in the ccntext of the eucharist, through the invocation of the Spirit and the laying on of hands as mandating and empowering the ordained for the responsibility of ministry in and for the community. The Lima text is quite elaborate on what it understands ordination to mean. In no less than five paragraphs, it elaborates on its central statement: "Ordination denotes an action by God and the community by which the ordained are strengthened by the Spirit for their task and are upheld by the acknowledgment and prayers of the congregation." [23]

The purpose for which the Commission on Faith and Order has set out upon formulating its understanding of the ordained ministry and ordination is to help the churches come to a mutual recognition of each other's ministry. The least this presupposes is that there is in the churches a shared understanding of the faith reality they are asked to recognize in each other. It is true, of course, that the argument for such a hoped-for recognition is not complete at this point, because I have not introduced as yet what the Faith and Order document has to say about the threefold pattern of that ordained ministry and more particularly about the episcopacy with which the thorny issue of apostolic succession is connected and which the episcopal churches consider essential to the recognition of ministry.

Before we proceed to that, it is legitimate to raise a question in light of the stated aim of these reflections on the ordained ministry: how will the churches come to a mutual recognition of each other's ministry? It is unrealistic to expect that it will be done in one complete act because that would in fact be tantamount to a reconciliation among the churches. Is it not more realistic to see such a goal realized in stages? And would not one such stage be that the churches at least recognize in each other the ordained ministry as soon as they are prepared to subscribe, both in theory and in practice, to the understanding of the ordained ministry and of ordination that is outlined here? Such a recognition will not be sufficient for a complete reconciliation between the churches, because in such a reconciliation there is obviously more at stake than what the ordained ministers in the local fellowship embody, but if we opt for a recognition in stages, then a recognition of what in fact is operative in the faith communities is a realistic way to start.

This seem to be the basic thrust of the Lima document when it states that "churches which have not retained the episcopate ... cannot accept any suggestion that the ministry exercised in their own tradition should be invalid until the moment that it enters into an existing line of episcopal succession." [24] Whether the introduction of the category of validity is an appropriate one is another matter; it is the more immediately available one, but some caution is called for in light of the different meanings validity can have. [25]

What the Lima statement is particularly concerned with is establishing the fact that "churches without the episcopal succession and living in faithful continuity with the apostolic faith and mission, have a ministry of Word and sacrament as is evident from the belief, practice and life of those churches." [26]

169

What is opted for in this position of the Lima document also resonates with the recommendation of the Roman Catholic/Lutheran Joint Commission in its 1981 report The Ministry in the Church:

> A mutual recognition that the ministry in the other church exercises essential functions of the ministry that Jesus Christ instituted in his church and, which one believes, is fully realized in one's own church. This as yet incomplete mutual recognition would include the affirmation that the Holy Spirit also operates in the other church through its ministries and makes use of these as means of salvation in the proclamation of the gospel, the administration of the sacraments, and the leadership of congregations. [27]

What this would mean for the Roman Catholic Church, for example, is at least that the ambiguous expression of Unitatis redintegratio referred to earlier must be understood in terms of a deficient ministry rather than a lack of ministry. This is also the orientation taken by the Roman Catholic participants in the Roman Catholic/Lutheran dialogue. [28] Such a recognition, however partial it may be, is all the more called for when there is a willingness on the part of the non-episcopal churches to at least investigate the possibility of recovering the episcopate for the sake of the ecclesial values that are embodied in it.

THE EPISCOPACY QUESTION

As is evident from the foregoing remarks, the real difficulty lies in what value must be ascribed to the historic episcopate, although we must be careful not to make this question absolute either. After all, the churches that have retained the historic episcopate do not even live in communion with each other, as is evidenced from the separation between the Roman Catholic Church and the Orthodox Church. The Lima document quite rightly reminds us of that when it suggests that the arguments for recovering the historic episcopate would be more convincing if "the episcopal churches themselves also regain their lost unity." [29]

The Lima document sets the question of the episcopate in the context of its reflections on the threefold pattern of bishop, presbyter and deacon. What is at issue here is "how the life of the Church is to be ordered," [30] particularly as this applies to

170

the forms of the ordained ministry. Placing it in an historical perspective, the churches today must come to terms with the fact that since the sixteenth century, in a number of places and communities, the functions of ordained ministry that since the second and third centuries had come to be distributed according to the threefold pattern of bishop, presbyter and deacon - a pattern that is still retained today by many churches - have come to be distributed according to structures other than the predominant threefold pattern. [31] This has resulted in the distinction between the non-episcopal and the episcopal churches, in which the state of dividedness between the churches in Western Christianity has expressed itself, at least in its more visible form. This division shows itself particularly in the governing polities they have developed, one being presbyteral-synodical, the other episcopal. These are structures that are basically intended to safeguard what each church considers to be important ecclesiological values.

In an attempt to resolve this division, the Lima document handles the situation differently than the bilateral dialogues. The latter have tended to explain that what in fact exists in the respective churches as far as the governing polity is concerned can be justified and entails important ecclesiological features. The Lima text mentions that approach as well, but its preference lies in placing the dilemma in the dynamic of the ecumenical movement, that is to say, in the common search for the visible unity that Christ willed and promised for his Church. In the perspective of the sought-for unity, the Lima document thus makes what amounts to a proposal, namely, to recover the historic episcopate, but at the same time it holds firm to four important facts: (1) there is no single New Testament pattern of ordained ministry; (2) the Spirit has led the Church to adapt its ministries to contextual needs many times; (3) other forms of the ordained ministry have been blessed with the gifts of the Holy Spirit; [32] and (4) churches without the historic episcopate have not been without a ministry of episkopē in some form. [33]

The present scandalous state of divisions between the churches and the search for visible unity may well constitute such a contextual need to which the Spirit urges the churches to respond in the form of recovering the threefold ministry: "The threefold ministry of bishop, presbyter and deacon may serve today as an expression of the unity we seek and also as a means of

achieving it." [34]   The proposal is repeated in yet
another way: "Churches not having the threefold pattern
... will further need to ask themselves whether the
threefold pattern as developed does not have a powerful
claim to be accepted by them." [35]   What is being
proposed here is that the threefold ministry begin to
serve as the basic structure of the ordained ministry
in the one re-united Church of the future.

Does this mean that the non-episcopal churches are
asked to cave in under pressure of the episcopal
churches and simply accept their polity?   It is not
quite that simple.   The Lima text may be straightfor-
ward in submitting its proposal, but it is equally
adamant in pointing out that the threefold ministry
proposed here will differ in significant ways from the
pattern that is in existence in the episcopal churches
today.   The point is that "the threefold pattern stands
in need of reform," [36] so that the "churches
maintaining the threefold pattern will need to ask how
its potential can be fully developed for the most
effective witness of the Church in this world." [37]
In other words, the burden is not only on the
non-episcopal but on the episcopal churches as well.

Moreover, one must not forget the historical fact
that the majority of the Reformation churches only
denied that the historic episcopate belongs to the
essence of the Church after their legitimate requests
for a much needed reform of the Church had fallen, in
the Reformers' estimation, on deaf ears.   It is felt
today that the degree of reform achieved in today's
episcopal churches is not sufficient to allow the
present form of the historic episcopate to be perceived
as a credible instrument and sign of the Church's
unity.

In order to help that much needed reform along,
the Lima document submits an outline of the basic
characteristics of such a reformed threefold pattern.
It will have to be an ordained ministry that is at the
same time personal, collegial and communal, and this
both at the local and at the regional level. [38]   In
other words, there must be structures that make
collegial and synodical procedures a reality, so that
the benefits gained from roughly four and a half
centuries of non-episcopal experience are not lost but
are integrated into a renewed form of the threefold
pattern.   It is difficult to say at this point whether
the repeated insistence on the recovery of the threefold pattern of bishop, presbyter and deacon is really

intended to include the recovery of the diaconate with
equal emphasis or whether that is a way of packaging
the proposal for recovering the episcopate. In the
light of what follows in the Lima document, I do not
think it is distorting its intent to give special
attention to the recovery of the episcopacy.

Acceptance of the episcopacy is not being proposed
as a matter of sociological convenience. It is being
proposed because a ministry of episkopē "is necessary
to express and safeguard the unity of the body. Every
church needs this ministry of unity in some form in
order to be the Church of God, the one Body of Christ,
a sign of the unity of all in the Kingdom." [39] This
is not to deny that in churches that have not retained
the form of historic episcopate "the reality and
function of the episcopal ministry have been preserved
in many of these churches, with or without the title
'bishop'," [40] but this ministry seems best expressed
when it is exercised in a personal way, "because the
presence of Christ among his people can most
effectively be pointed to by the person ordained to
proclaim the Gospel and to call the community to serve
the Lord in unity of life and witness." [41]

What lies behind this proposal to recover the
historic episcopate are some ecclesiological considerations that the Lima document has not articulated as
well as one might have wished and that would have given
its proposal more weight. As mentioned earlier, the
starting point for the document's reflections on the
ordained ministry was the place and role of the ordained ministry in the more immediate experience of
ecclesial fellowship at the local level. The question
is what about the link or bond of a given local community with other local communities? Is the Church not
actualized as well in the bond between the local
communities and is there not a need for a unique
ministry at that level too? The churches of the
Catholic type speak of church - in terms of diocese -
as the communion of the local eucharistic communities
and hold the "office bearer," the bishop, as the
ordained minister whose primary ministry it is to serve
the unity among the local eucharistic communities. On
this basis the episcopacy is considered as an inherent-
ly constitutive reality of the Church. These are
considerations that the Roman Catholic/Lutheran document on the ministry has made more explicit:

> The church is actualized at different
> levels: as the local church (congregation),

as the church of a larger region or country,
and as the universal church. At each of
these levels, albeit in different forms,
it is essential that the ministry be both
the 'in and over against' the ecclesial
community. [42]

Since we mention here the Roman Catholic/Lutheran
dialogue, it is interesting to note that while its
document on the ordained ministry refrains from making
a recommendation concerning the episcopacy, its
document Ways to Community has not been so reticent:

> According to Lutheran understanding the
> individual congregation is essentially
> related to the church as a whole. There
> is a need beyond the local congregation
> for leadership services (episcopē) with
> pastoral responsibility for proclamation,
> sacraments and church unity. Thus, in
> addition to the office of parish pastor,
> there is a place for supracongregational
> ministries in the church. Although
> Lutherans do not regard the historic
> episcopacy as based on an explicit
> irrevocable command from the Lord valid
> for all times and situations, yet this
> polity arose through the work of the
> Holy Spirit and there are historical and
> ecumenical reasons for seriously considering
> its restoration in Lutheran churches. [43]

The concern that gives rise to this recommendation is
again the reality of Church beyond the local level:

> Just as the pastoral practice of ordained
> parish clergy is of great importance on the
> local level, so that actualization of
> ministries of church leadership beyond the
> congregational level is of decisive
> significance for possible mutual readiness
> to enter the fellowship of the historic
> episcopacy... . [44]

The rather disappointing silence by the Lima
document concerning these ecclesiological considerations manifests one of its weakest points: an as-yet
underdeveloped ecclesiology. As it stands, hardly any
attention is given to the communion among the churches
in which the bishops exercise their ministry of
episkopē. This weakness in the Lima document is

somewhat surprising, if one considers the influence the Groupe des Dombes has otherwise had on the work of Faith and Order. [45] What is underdeveloped is the question of episcopal collegiality and in connection with that the teaching authority of the bishops in the Church, a question about which the Lima document remains silent as well. [46] On this point, the Lima document might significantly benefit from an attempt to integrate some of the ecclesiological considerations that have made their way into the introduction to ARCIC's Final Report. The latter document gives a brief outline of the communion ecclesiology that underlies its reflections on the eucharist, ministry and authority. [47] It is all part of the growing awareness that, however necessary it is to deal with the question of ordained ministry, ecclesiology cannot be avoided. It may well turn out to be the decisive issue in the end.

This particular aspect of the ministry of episkopē is only hesitantly referred to when the Lima text describes the function of the bishops: "They relate the Christian community in their area to the wider Church, and the universal Church to their community." [48] It would be difficult to maintain that this brief reference has given sufficient attention to the catholicity of the Church, to which the college of bishops relates in a significant way. In fact, it is safe to say that the catholic dimension of the Church has been largely ignored in the Lima text. Could the reason for the virtual absence of this dimension be that, if it were to be articulated more extensively, eventually the possibility of a Petrine ministry, with its unique place within the college of bishops with which it is supposed to serve the unity of the universal Church, would have to be considered? [49] The latter issue was raised at Lima, but it was considered too significant an issue to be dealt with in a hasty manner. [50] Roman Catholic theologians might have been expected to introduce this particular dimension into the search for unity. Their relatively late arrival at the Faith and Order Commission in the late 1960s may partly explain why there is no mention whatsoever of the Petrine ministry in the Lima text on the ordained ministry. It may be added that the shape this ministry has taken in the course of the centuries in the form of the papacy cannot be very inviting. Of course, it would have to be drastically reformed before it could ever be considered seriously. However, the churches not having the episcopacy are invited to participate in its reform. [51] Perhaps the churches that cannot accept

175

the Petrine ministry should likewise be invited to participate in the latter's reform. Such an assistance might also be of great benefit to the tradition that has the Petrine ministry in the form of the papacy.

APOSTOLIC SUCCESSION [52]

To serve the unity or bond among the different local communities and to actualize the reality of the Church at a wider-than-local level is only one aspect of the role of the bishops. A second equally important aspect of that role is to maintain and serve the link or continuity with the communities of the past. Continuity in the apostolic faith, continuity with the Church of the apostles, is inherent to the reality of the Church. It is also from this perspective that the Lima text asks the churches without episcopal succession to recover the sign of episcopal succession because it is felt that "the continuity with the Church of the apostles finds profound expression in the successive laying on of hands by bishops and that ... this sign will strengthen and deepen that continuity." [53]

We touch here upon another delicate issue that is often described as apostolic succession. To whom or to what must apostolic succession be ascribed? Is apostolic succession to be identified with episcopal succession in the sense of the transmission of the episcopal office going back in an unbroken chain to the apostles? On the surface this seems to be the position of the episcopal churches. We may even find remnants of it in the recent first document of the Joint International Commission for theological dialogue between the Roman Catholic Church and the Orthodox Church. It says: "The bishop receives the gift of episcopal grace (1 Tim. 4:14) in the sacrament of consecration effected by bishops who themselves have received this gift, thanks to the existence of an uninterrupted series of episcopal ordinations, beginning from the holy apostles." [54] In all fairness, it must be said that the same document in the following paragraph gives an interpretation of this expression which is more compatible with the way the Lima text handles the question of apostolic succession.

What has happened ecumenically with the question of apostolic succession is a restating of the issue so that it is no longer narrowly thought of in terms of ministerial office only. This is precisely what the Lima text does. A distinction is made between the

176

Church's succession in the apostolic tradition and succession of the apostolic ministry. Succession in the apostolic tradition means:

> continuity in the permanent characteristics of the Church of the apostles: witness to the apostolic faith, proclamation and fresh interpretation of the Gospel, celebration of baptism and the eucharist, the transmission of ministerial responsibilities, communion in prayer, love, joy and suffering, service to the sick and the needy, unity among the local churches and sharing the gifts which the Lord has given to each. The primary manifestation of apostolic succession is to be found in the apostolic tradition of the Church as a whole. The succession is an expression of the permanence and, therefore, of the continuity of Christ's own mission in which the Church participates. [55]

This is what the Roman Catholic/Lutheran document calls the apostolic succession in terms of its content: "the apostolicity of the Church in faith." [56] And it continues: "The whole Church as the ecclesia apostolica stands in the apostolic succession." [57]

Once that is clearly affirmed, the proper setting is provided for the succession of the apostolic ministry, because as the commentary to paragraph 34 explains: "Within this apostolic tradition is an apostolic succession of the ministry which serves the continuity of the Church in its life in Christ and its faithfulness to the words and acts of Jesus transmitted by the apostles." [58] In other words, the succession in ministry must be seen in relation to the apostolic faith of the Church that the ordained ministry is called upon to preserve and actualize. In that light, the ordained ministry can legitimately be understood as being called to be the guardian of the faith. [59] What the Lima text does here is take ministerial succession out of its isolation and re-appreciate it as a clearly ecclesial reality.

What must be noted here is that the Lima text, in describing the relationship between ministerial succession and the apostolicity of the Church, carefully avoids equating ministerial succession with episcopal succession. Whether it thereby opts for what some have called a presbyteral succession, by which ministerial succession would have been preserved in the Reformation churches as well, is not entirely clear. Apart from the fact that the question formulated in these terms has a tendency to once again isolate ministerial succession from its properly ecclesial context, if pressed for it in these terms, the Lima response might well be affirmative. Or the least it would maintain is that, because of the absence of episcopal succession, it cannot be argued that churches without the historic episcopate have thereby automatically ceased to live in faithful continuity with the apostolic faith and mission. Churches that have maintained episcopal succession are asked to recognize that fact. [60]

However, the Lima document does not stay at this level of the debate. It is more concerned with what needs to be done today if the visible unity of the Church is to be restored. This does not mean that it considers the historical question inappropriate; it is more a matter of giving priority to the search for unity in the midst of the present condition of division and to the demands that come from restoring the unity. In that light, the Lima document holds that episcopal succession has much to commend itself. While such succession cannot claim to be the only way in which the apostolic tradition of the Church is expressed, it can be understood, as it was understood in the earlier period of the Church's history, "as serving, symbolizing and guarding the continuity of the apostolic faith and communion." [61] Since episcopal succession can thus be appreciated "as a sign, though not a guarantee, of the continuity and unity of the Church," [62] or "as a sign of the apostolicity of the life of the whole Church," [63] the Lima document does not hesitate to make the following recommendation:

> Churches without the episcopal succession ... are asked to realize that the continuity with the Church of the apostles finds profound expression in the successive laying on of hands by bishops and that, though they may not lack the continuity of the apostolic tradition, this sign will strengthen and deepen that continuity. They may need to recover the sign of the episcopal succession. [64]

It is also under this aspect of succession in the apostolic tradition signified and served by episcopal succession that the Lima document could find a broader base of support in a more developed communion ecclesiology. The episcopal succession it recommends stands too isolated. This could easily be corrected if the Lima document were to be attentive to a practice of the episcopal churches whereby, in the ordination ceremony, neighboring bishops, as witnesses of the apostolic faith of their own churches, lay hands on a new bishop thereby inserting the latter with his church into the communion of local churches that recognize and affirm each other in the apostolic faith. [65] This orientation would prevent episcopal succession from being understood in a physical and narrowly linear-historical sense and would bring out more forcefully the communion with other apostolic churches.

In retrospect, there are basically two complementary and interlocking reasons why the Lima document recommends the acceptance of the historic episcopate. These two reasons, on the one hand, flow immediately from two constitutive features that mark the life of the Church, namely unity and apostolicity, and, on the other hand, shape the special responsibility of the episcopal office, which serves the Church's unity and apostolicity. These are, in other words, not isolated ministerial prerogatives that substantiate the recommendation of the Lima text, but rather decisive ecclesial values without which the Church cannot be Church. This is not to suggest that these values, because of the absence of the historic episcopate, have been entirely lacking in the life of the Church, but they have been seriously impaired on account of it, if one judges by the state of division in the Church. This applies as well to the Church's catholicity which, as mentioned earlier, has not received the attention it deserves in the document. While it is obvious that, in the final analysis, it is the Spirit of the Risen One, who maintains the Church of Christ in unity, apostolicity and catholicity, [66] he does not work without historical mediations.

CONCLUSION

The Lima document addresses other matters besides that of the episcopacy, including such issues as the designation of ordained ministers as priests [67] and the ordination of women. [68] I believe, however, that the recovery of the episcopacy presents the churches at the present time with quite a sufficient amount of material upon which to reflect and act. The Commission on Faith and Order speaks to a wide-ranging constituency. It presumably feels that its own thinking on the question of the ordained ministry has sufficiently matured to enable it to submit its text, together with the texts on baptism and on eucharist, to the member churches not just for comment, but for "an official response to this text at the highest appropriate level of authority." [69]

Perhaps I have given a disproportionate amount of attention to the text's proposal to recover the episcopacy, but, as I understand it, the proposal is formulated in such a way that it asks for just as much conversion and reform on the part of the episcopal churches as it does on the part of the non-episcopal churches. It would, therefore, be a sad mistake, if not in fact a shirking of ecumenical responsibilities, if the Roman Catholic Church were to become a mere spectator to the response of the other churches to the Lima document. The least that can be asked of the Roman Catholic Church is that it recognize the ordained ministry of the Reformation churches, even if it can only be a partial recognition at this point, and that it reform its own ordained ministry in such a way as to enable it to begin to function in a personal, collegial and communal way at the local level, at the universal level and at every level in between.

What the Commission on Faith and Order is entitled to receive after fifty-nine years of groping and searching is an indication of whether the churches are prepared, on theological grounds that can be strengthened still further, to follow the path suggested, or whether we must set out in search of another way to arrive at some form of visible unity for Christ's Church.

Notes for Chapter X

The present article is a modified version of "The Lima Document on the Ordained Ministry: A Challenge to All the Churches," Eglise et théologie 14 (1983) 131-53, reproduced here with permission.

1. Baptism, Eucharist and Ministry (Faith and Order Paper 111; Geneva: WCC, 1982) 19-32. References to this text will be abbreviated as Lima M.

2. For an overview of these dialogues, see William Marrevee, "Emerging Ecumenical Consensus on the Ordained Ministry," Eglise et théologie 11 (1980) 195-222 and 399-419.

3. To resolve the potential uneasiness, the Commission on Faith and Order initiated a forum on the bilateral conversations. The result of this forum is The Three Reports of the Forum on Bilateral Conversations (Faith and Order Paper 107; Geneva: WCC, 1981) 52. See also: Fourth Forum of Bilateral Conversations for the meeting held in 1985.

4. Georg H. Vischer, Apostolischer Dienst: Fünfzig Jahre Diskussion über das kirchliche Amt in Glauben und Kirchenverfassung (Frankfurt: Otto Lembeck, 1982). Cf. Kuncheria Pathil, Models in Ecumenical Dialogue: A Study of the Methodological Development in the Commission of 'Faith and Order' of the World Council of Churches (Bangalore: Dharmaram, 1981).

5. H. Denzinger - A. Schönmetzer, Enchiridion Symbolorum (Freiburg: Herder, 1963) no. 3315-19.

6. Unitatis redintegratio, no. 22.

7. Unitatis redintegratio, no. 15.

8. One Baptism, One Eucharist and a Mutually Recognized Ministry (Faith and Order Paper 73; Geneva: WCC, 1975) 64.

9. Lima M51-55.

10. Lima M6.

11. Lima M5 and 8.

12. Lima M8.

13. Lima M12.

14. Lima M8.

15. Lima M12.

16. Lima M14.

17. Lima M12.

18. Lima M15.

19. Lima M16.

20. Lima M13.

21. Lima M15.

22. Lima M11 and 10.

23. Lima M40; 39-44; 15.

24. Lima M38.

25. John A. Gurrieri, "Sacramental Validity: The Origins and Use of Vocabulary," The Jurist 41 (1981) 21-58.

26. Lima M53b.

27. The Joint Lutheran/Roman Catholic Study Commission, "The Ministry in the Church," Origins 11 (1982) 295-304, par. 85. References to this text will be abbreviaetd as L-RC M.

28. L-RC M 75-78. It is a position earlier put forward by the Lutheran/Roman Catholic Dialogue in the United States: Paul Empie and T. Austin Murphy, eds., Lutherans and Catholics in Dialogue: IV, Eucharist and Ministry, St. Louis, 1970 (Minneapolis: Augsburg, 1971) par. 54-59. A Catholic Theological Society of America Study Committee has raised objections to such recognition as supposedly lacking sufficient grounds. Catholic Theological Society of America, "The Bilateral Consultations between the Roman Catholic Church in the United Church and other Christian Communions," in CTSA, Proceedings 27 (1972) 200-02. Carl Peter shares that opinion "Rome and the Ministry of Other Churches," Ecumenical Trends 9 (1980) 6. However, I believe that Harry McSorley is correct in his disagreement with this negative assessment: "Roman Catholic Recognition of

Protestant Ministries," Ecumenical Trends 10 (1981) 97-100; "Determining the 'Validity' of Orders and the Meaning of 'Validity'," The Jurist 41 (1981) 371-404. See also: Franz Josef van Beeck, Grounded in Love (Washington: University Press of America, 1981) especially 75-124.

29. Lima M38.

30. Lima M6.

31. Lima M19-22.

32. Lima M22.

33. Lima M19 and 53a.

34. Lima M22.

35. Lima M25.

36. Lima M24.

37. Lima M25.

38. Lima M26-27. Note that what is proposed here is more than an echo of what COCU proposed in its revised chapter on Ministry. Consultation on Church Union, In Quest of a Church of Christ Uniting (Princeton: COCU, 1980) 39-46.

39. Lima M23.

40. Lima M37.

41. Lima M26.

42. L-RC M45.

43. The Joint Lutheran/Roman Catholic Study Commission, "Ways to Community," One in Christ 17 (1981) 356-87, par. 23. References to this text will be abbreviated as L-RC WC.

44. L-RC WC88.

45. Groupe des Dombes, "The Episcopal Ministry," One in Christ 14 (1978) 267-88.

46. Cf., L-RC M50-58.

47. The Final Report, Introduction, par. 4-9.

48. Lima M29.

49. Some promising work has in fact been done already on the ecumenical level: ARCIC, "Authority in the Church," in The Final Report, 49-98; Paul Empie and T. Austin Murphy, eds., Lutherans and Catholics in Dialogues: V: Papal Primacy and the Universal Church (Minneapolis: Augsburg, 1974) 9-42. Even the International Lutheran/Roman Catholic report, without treating the question exhaustively at this point, has some encouraging remarks to make on it: L-RC M3 and 67-73; L-RC WC23. See also: Michael Hardt, Papsttum und Ökumene: Ansätze eines Neuverständnisses für einen Papstprimat in der protestantischen Theologie des 20. Jahrhunderts (Paderborn: Schöningh, 1981) 162; Jean-Marie Tillard, The Bishop of Rome (London: SPCK, 1983).

50. Michael Kinnamon, ed., Towards Visible Unity, Vol.1, 82.

51. Lima M25.

52. For a significant study of this aspect of the Lima document see: Werner Löser, "Die Gegenwart Jesu Christi und die Apostolizität der Kirche - ein katholischer Beitrag zur Rezeption der Konvergenzerklärung 'Das Amt' (Lima 1982)," Theologie und Philosophie 59 (1984) 379-92.

53. Lima M53b.

54. Joint International Commission for Theological Dialogue Between the Roman Catholic Church and the Orthodox Church, "The Mystery of the Church and of the Eucharist in the Light of the Mystery of the Holy Trinity," Origins 11 (1982) 157-60, Chapter II, par. 3. References to this text are abbreviated as RC-O M.

55. Lima M34-35.

56. L-RC M59.

57. L-RC M61.

58. Lima M34 Commentary.

59. Lima M35.

60. Lima M53a and 37.

61. Lima M36.

62. Lima M38.

63. Ibid.

64. Lima M53b.

65. RC-O MII, 4; ARCIC M16.

66. Lima M34.

67. Lima M17 and Commentary.

68. Lima M18 and Commentary.

69. Lima, Preface, p. X.

SELECTED BIBLIOGRAPHY

Michael A. Fahey

TEXT OF THE LIMA DOCUMENT:

Baptism, Eucharist and Ministry. Faith and Order
    Paper 111. Geneva: World Council of Churches,
    1982.

Growth in Agreement: Reports and Agreed Statements of
    Ecumenical Conversations on a World Level. eds.,
    Harding Meyer and Lukas Vischer. Faith and Order
    Paper 108. Geneva: World Council of Churches; New
    York: Paulist, 1984, pp. 465-503.

BIBLIOGRAPHY:

Puglisi, James G. and Voicu, Sever J., A Bibliography
    of Interchurch and Interconfessional Theological
    Dialogues. Rome: Centro pro Unione, 1984.
    Available from the Centro pro Unione, Via
    dell'Anima 30; I-00186 Rome, Italy.

COMMENTARIES, STUDY GUIDES:

"An Agreed Statement on the Lima Document by the
    Eastern Orthodox/Roman Catholic Consultation, USA,
    1984," Greek Orthodox Theological Review 29 (1984)
    283-88.

"Baptism, Eucharist and Ministry and its Reception in
    the U.S. Churches," ed., J. Gros. Journal of
    Ecumenical Studies 21, no. 1 (1984), entire issue.
    Also published as a separate volume under the same
    title by Pilgrim Press, Boston.

Baptism and Eucharist: Ecumenical Convergence in
    Celebration. eds., Max Thurian and Geoffrey
    Wainwright. Faith and Order Paper 117. Grand
    Rapids: Eerdmans; Geneva: World Council of
    Churches, 1983.

Churches Respond: Some Examples of How the Churches are
    Reacting to the Baptism, Eucharist and Ministry
    Text. ed., Max Thurian. Faith and Order Paper 129.
    Geneva: World Council of Churches, 1985.

Ecumenical Perspectives on Baptism, Eucharist and
    Ministry. ed., Max Thurian. Faith and Order Paper
    116. Geneva: World Council of Churches, 1983.

Etudes théologiques et religieuses (Montpelier, France)
58, no. 2 (1983). Four articles on BEM.

Evangelical Anglicans and the Lima Text: An Assessment
and Critique. ed., T. Price. Grove Worship Series
92. Bramcote, Notts.: Grove Books, 1985.

"Foi et Constitution" La Conférence de Lima," Istina
27, no. 1 (1982), entire issue.

Fourth Forum of Bilateral Conversations: Reports.
Faith and Order Paper 125. Geneva: World Council
of Churches, 1985. Report of the meeting, March
5-9, 1985 to compare the findings of BEM with the
various bilateral consensus statements. See esp.
pp. 9-11 for a list of nine points of convergence.

International Review of Missions 72 (April 1983)
153-266. Issue devoted to BEM. See esp. article
by Indian Jesuit, Samuel Rayan, 199-206.

Kinnamon, Michael. Why It Matters: A Popular
Introduction to the Baptism, Eucharist and
Ministry Text. Risk Book 25. Geneva: World
Council of Churches, 1985.

Kommentar zu den Lima-Erklärungen über Taufe,
Eucharistie und Amt. ed., Konfessionskundliches
Institut, Bensheimer Heft 59; Göttingen:
Vandenhoeck and Ruprecht, 1983.

Lazareth, William H., Growing Together in Baptism,
Eucharist and Ministry: A Study Guide. Faith and
Order Paper 114. Geneva: World Council of
Churches, 1982.

"The Lima Document," in Ecumenism (Montreal) No. 70
(June) 1983, entire issue.

La Maison Dieu no. 163 (1985), entire issue, containing
papers of the Societas Liturgica meeting, Boston,
1985.

Mid-Stream: An Ecumenical Journal 23, no. 3 (July
1984). A special issue devoted to enabling the
study and reception of Baptism, Eucharist and
Ministry.

Orthodox Perspectives on Baptism, Eucharist and
Ministry. Faith and Order Paper 128. Geneva:
World Council of Churches, 1985. Originally

published as a special issue of Greek Orthodox
Theological Review 30, no. 2 (1985) which
contains the papers from an international
inter-Orthodox symposium held on BEM in 1985.

St. Vladimir's Theological Quarterly 27, no. 4 (1983),
entire issue.

"Tenth International Congress of Jesuit Ecumenists,
Oxford, July 14-18, 1985," The Month n.s. 18
(October 1985). Entire issue on the theme: "ARCIC
Final Report and BEM."

Towards a Church of England Response to BEM and ARCIC.
ed., Church of England, Board for Mission and
Unity. London: CIO, 1985.

PUBLICATIONS BY INDIVIDUAL AUTHORS:

Bachiocchi, J. de, "Les ministères ecclésiaux dans le
texte de Lima: Baptême, Eucharistie, Ministère
(Foi et Constitution, début 1982)." Mélanges de
science religieuse 40 (1983) 73-90.

Cornélis, Jérôme, "Jalons sur la route de l'unité,"
Unité des Chrétiens No. 47 (juillet 1982) 26-39.

Dantine, Johannes, "Zur Konvergenzerklärung über Taufe,
Eucharistie und Amt, Lima 1982," Oekumenische
Rundschau 32 (1983) 12-27.

Dulles, Avery, "Toward a Christian Consensus: The Lima
Meeting," America 146 (1982) 126-29.

Eagan, Joseph F., S.J., "Ordained Ministry in BEM: A
Theological Critique," Ecumenical Review 36 (1984)
263-77.

Fries, Heinrich, and Rahner, Karl, Unity of the
Churches - An Actual Possibility. Philadelphia:
Fortress, 1983.

Hastings, C.B., "The Lima Document: A Southern Baptist
View," Ecumenical Trends 12, no. 2 (Feb. 1983)
24-27.

Kilmartin, Edward, J., "A Catholic Response to Lima
1982," Centro pro Unione, Bulletin No. 27 (Spring
1985) 8-16. Also in One in Christ 21 (1985)
204-16.

Löser, Werner, S.J., "Die Gegenwart Jesu Christi und die Apostolizität der Kirche - ein katholischer Beitrag zur Rezeption der Konvergenzerklärung 'Das Amt' (Lima 1982)," Theologie und Philosophie 59 (1984) 379-92.

Reumann, John, The Supper of the Lord: The New Testament, Ecumenical Dialogues, and Faith and Order on Eucharist. Philadelphia: Fortress, 1985.

Salado Martinez, Domingo, "La doctrina eucarística en el documento de Lima 1982," Diálogo Ecuménico 18 (1983) 79-122.

Thurian, Max, The Mystery of the Eucharist: An Ecumenical Approach. trans. by Emily Chisholm. Grand Rapids: Eerdmans, 1984. = Le mystère de l'Eucharistie, 1981.

Vischer, Lukas, "Rezeption in der ökumenischen Bewegung: Die Texte über Taufe, Eucharistie und Amt," Kerygma und Dogma 29 (1983) 86-99.

Voss, Gerhard, "Das Lima Dokument 'Taufe, Eucharistie und Amt' in katholischer Sicht," Catholica 36 (1982) 181-94.

DATE DUE

JAN 5 '90			
SEP 16			
APR 3 0 2002			
DEC 3 0 2009			